Drawn Fabric Embroidery

Drawn Fabric Embroidery

Edna Wark

B T Batsford Limited   London

First published 1979
First published in paperback 1987
ISBN 0 7134 1477 4

Filmset in 'Monophoto' Apollo by
Servis Filmsetting Limited, Manchester
Printed in Great Britain by
The Anchor Press Ltd, Tiptree, Essex
for the publishers
B T Batsford Limited
4 Fitzhardinge Street, London W1H 0AH

Contents

Acknowledgment

I wish to thank a number of people who have helped in the production of this book – especially Mary-Ellen Belville who has made many of the black and white photographic prints, except numbers 1, 29 and 44 and those supplied by museum sources; my friends from overseas who sent photographs of their work to me and the other friends who allowed me to photograph their work – much of which was not used for one reason or another. Their interest and encouragement has meant a great deal to me. Any photographs or work not acknowledged in the text are my own.

My thanks also go to the Departments of Photography and the Media, of the Melbourne State College, who gave me access to their darkrooms; to Winifred Clayton, London, with whom I did my first drawn fabric sampler; to Gertie Wandel, Copenhagen, who took me to her home, gave me advice from her great store of wisdom and allowed me to photograph samplers in her collection.

Permission was given to me by the Embroiderers' Guild, Victoria, to use material contained in a folio of my work which is in their possession and to photograph pieces in their collection, for which I thank them.

The National Gallery of Victoria in Melbourne, the Victoria and Albert Museum of London, the Kunstindustrimuseet of Copenhagen and the Norfolk Museums Services have let me use photographs supplied by them and the Industrie-und-Gewerbe-Museum in St Gall, Switzerland, kindly allowed me to take my own photographs.

Without my 'Man Friday', whose name is William, this book would probably never have been started. He has taken part at every stage; and it is dedicated to:
all my fellow-embroiderers who love drawn fabric embroidery

Foreword

In writing this book I have had two aims in mind. In 1976 I set aside time to study drawn fabric embroidery in some depth. I enjoyed my studies so much that I decided to share them with others. My second aim has been to make information available to embroiderers in those parts of the world where they do not have the advantages of their European counterparts of being able to visit museums with large collections of historical exhibits.

When early settlers came to Australia their luggage was filled with items important for everyday survival and historic embroideries did not fall into that category. Use of a needle in any form was unknown to the native Australian so there was no indigenous embroidery to be seen.

I have included photographs of some work done currently in Australia to let readers elsewhere see that there are embroiderers working in this part of the world. Early teachers all came from Britain and present day ones are greatly influenced by the many books which are published in England and America, so that fashions and trends in Australian embroidery are mainly the same as in other parts of the English-speaking world.

I have also included as much information as I can about where drawn fabric embroideries may be seen. Australians are great travellers and there is so much to be seen if one only knows where to look. The two collections of which I know in Australia, are unknown to most Australians or anyone else.

In visiting museums for the express purpose of seeing specific embroideries it is as well to contact the museum in question before visiting. Some things are not on permanent display and an appointment is needed. Also, my experience has been that, if space is required for extra exhibitions, the first things likely to be put away are the embroideries. After all, in most cases, they pack away easily.

I have not attempted to include a complete vocabulary of stitches. In the main, the stitches used are the stitches used in other techniques but given a tighter tension and worked on looser fabric. For further information about stitches, I refer readers to the very good book written by Moyra McNeill to whose teaching I owe a great deal. I think the other books on which we have relied for years are all out of print, although available from many good libraries. They are by Kate Lofthouse, Etta Campbell, Mrs Archibald Christie and Agnes Leach.

Thelma M Nye of Batsford, was kind enough to suggest that she thought that there was a place for a book such as this and suggested ways in which the original draft could be expanded to become of wider interest. I am most grateful for her help and encouragement.

E W
Canterbury, Victoria, Australia 1979

1 *Trees* 21 × 19 cm (8½ × 7½ in.)
Constance Howard, London
Photograph by Paul D Scott

Introduction

Drawn fabric embroidery or pulled thread embroidery – it is known by both names – should not be confused with drawn thread embroidery. In the first method no threads are withdrawn in the working. In the second many threads are withdrawn. In either case it may be used in conjunction with other techniques. Many of today's best workers prefer to use and mix techniques in a wonderfully rich and free way (*1*).

And what if every second thread in the weft is withdrawn? You have weft threads detached from the warp and they are either in front of or behind it (*2*). If you withdraw alternate threads from warp *and* weft, the warp threads and weft threads will be completely separate, one in front of the other and you can draw them into contrasting patterns in either case. Here we are really in the realm of needleweaving.

If some of the threads are withdrawn in a particular area of the fabric, in a traditional way, the work done on the looser areas is still drawn fabric. It is only when the withdrawal of the threads in a particular area completely alters the character of the fabric, that classification is altered.

For the purposes of this book, I have concerned myself only with stitches and work done on fabrics with warp and weft interlaced. Traditionally, these fabrics are linen (of varying degrees of coarseness) and very fine muslin.

Again traditionally, threads should be about the same thickness as the individual threads of the fabric. They need to be strong to maintain the tension and to withstand the pulling. They should be sufficiently tightly twisted not to fluff. For this reason, short lengths are preferable to lengthy pulling back and forth through the fabric. They should be of self-colour (not necessarily white on white) for greatest effect. Neutral shades on cream can be attractive, however. Alterations in scale or spacing of stitches can provide interesting variations.

French knots, used more in the past than today, and chain and stem stitches, whether simple or whipped or raised, all have their place. However, the joy of this technique is clean, uncluttered lines and sufficient unworked area to give a feeling of space. Remember though that the shapes of the free areas are just as important as the shapes in the design.

Free drawn fabric which can be developed directly onto the fabric, holds no limitations to the stitch variety that can be used, and experimentation with well-known stitches in different-weight threads, and threads with different surface finishes, can produce most attractive and unusual results.

For completion of table linen, there are hems with mitred corners, with or without decoration. There are also lacy edgings, surprisingly durable in their fragile appearance, worked in four-sided stitch with a picot edge and satin stitch rows or blocks. The combination of four-sided stitch can be in groups – irregular or regular – as long as it looks as if the irregularities were intended. There is a pitfall to be avoided, the satin stitch rows or blocks should be worked first, otherwise it can be very difficult to get the needle between every thread, after they have been drawn together into four-sided stitch. Then one can return and finish the four-sided stitches where required.

The ability to count is a decided advantage and meticulous attention to the counting is essential. If a basic denominator of 12 threads is used, stitches using 2, 3, 4 or 6 threads can be included. If a large area has to be counted, as in a table-cloth, start counting from the centre and place a pin at every 24 threads. It helps to keep the tally correct.

Experimental work, where areas are to be very open and tightly pulled, is easier if worked in a frame.

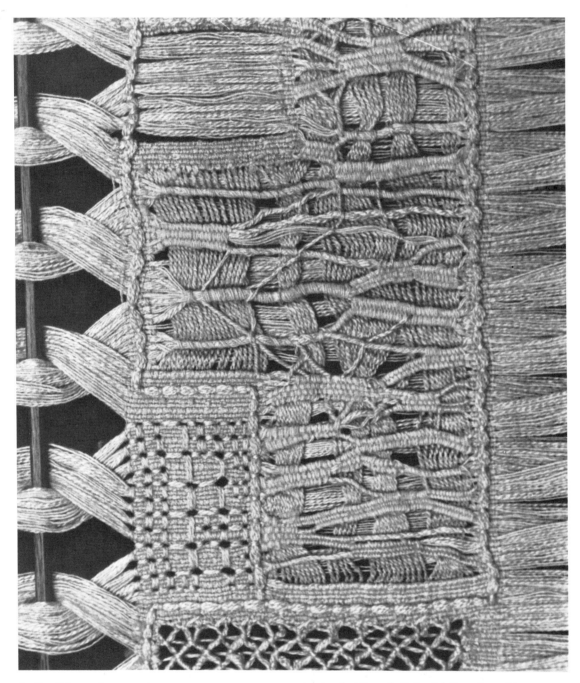

2 Detail from a large panel
Cynthia Singer, London
Alternate weft threads have been withdrawn in some
areas. The withdrawn threads have been used to do
the embroidery giving complete harmony to the work

3 Casalguidi work. Pale pink linen bag with
embroidery in high relief in white
Embroiderers' Guild Collection, Melbourne

12

Some stitches work best in straight rows or blocks, some in a diagonal pattern. Some are completed in one working movement; some need, or are easier done, half one way and completed on the way back.

Sometimes it is possible to get similar effects with different stitches. There is probably a good reason for the diversity. For instance, it is possible to produce a squared stitch suitable for grounding, that has no threads crossing at the back, as in four-sided stitch. It is also possible to produce a diagonal line stitch which looks like double faggot but without the diagonal stitch on the back. Both variations would be ideal on something where the embroidery needs to look the same on both sides. Turkish embroidery has this characteristic.

Historical examples in Europe and England are almost always worked in scroll designs, in which there are many small areas, giving scope for the use of many different stitches in the various areas; but how suitable these stitches are for contemporary designs of lines and rectangles! Nevertheless, it is quite possible to create circles or the impression of circles, the eye can be easily led. Eyelets, particularly the squared variety, and parts of eyelets, are so right in this setting. They can be massed with great effect.

Satin stitch on the counted thread, can give light and shade by changing the direction of the stitch groups. Satin stitch can also give changes in density by pulling some groups tightly and leaving some groups without tension, when just working over the same number of threads in a straight row.

Drawn fabric designs can be either positive or negative. If the ground is drawn into an open mesh and the design left unworked it is negative. If the design is worked and the background left unworked it is positive. There are parallels of this in other techniques. With cross stitch, it may be either the design which is worked, or if the design is voided and the background filled in, it is known as Assisi work.

The single most important factor to be learnt in drawn fabric embroidery is the control of stitch tension.

Sorbello work uses a beautiful, simple knotted stitch to fill in the design solidly and is sometimes done in conjunction with a drawn background (46).

Casalguidi work uses squared ground stitches for the background and the designs are in bold raised stem stitch and detached lace stitches (3).

History of embroidery with special reference to drawn fabric

The origin of embroidery is lost in the story of civilisation but if we agree with the idea that embroidery is essentially plain sewing turned into a work of art, by countless generations of men and women who loved stitches and experimented with them, we probably have the story in a nutshell.

From the essential joining of small skins and later, narrow widths of hand-woven materials, came ornamental lines of stitching, sometimes leaving a lacy pattern, such as faggoting, and sometimes close and ornamented, as with feather-stitching.

Earliest needles were of animal or fish-bone, then of iron, then steel and finally of stainless steel or other rustless finishes. Threads which in their earliest forms were animal sinews, became twisted fibres of wool, cotton, linen or silk and today are frequently man-made. The strength and fineness of threads has not necessarily become better as the centuries have passed. Today, for instance, we cannot get the fine sewing threads that were available 100 years ago. And the beautiful, fine, silky muslins which were used for the basis of the superb drawn fabric embroidery made in the eighteenth century and which, truly, rivalled the lace of the time, are no more.

In the beginning, materials and threads for making up and for ornamentation would have been the product of the family unit. Then, by means of barter and trade, they became an asset which formed part of the family's income.

There are records of elaborate embroidery from pre-Biblical times in Ur and Egypt. In the Bible, instructions were given for the garments of the priests and the furnishing of the Ark of the Testimonies, in coloured and gold embroidery. The embroiderer, a male, was an important member of the Jewish community of the Old Testament.

Relics found in Egyptian tombs have been richly embroidered and re-constructions of ceremonial tents show linings and curtains of 'patched' work, stitched together and embroidered.

In Saxon times in England, queens were skilled needlewomen and ecclesiastical relics are attributed to various members of royal families. Edward the Confessor's wife embroidered his coronation mantle, we are told.

Embroidery is a craft which goes hand-in-hand with other forms of ornamentation in every period. It cannot stand on its own because it must go 'in' something or be an adjunct 'to' something. It is only recently that anyone has tried to make embroidery 'free standing', although the various pieces which made up stump work were made in the round and then assembled. Stump work came in packages containing all the pieces that were needed and was a forerunner of today's 'kits'.

The monarchs of England have had great influence on the richness of English embroideries. The garments worn by Henry VIII and Elizabeth I set a pattern of opulence with a wealth of detail in stitch, detailed pattern and embellishment with jewels which today leaves us breathless.

By the seventeenth century, life in England was becoming less rigorous with the introduction of window glazing. It is hard to appreciate fully what this must have meant. Amongst other things, it meant that a completely different style of architecture could develop. There were now windows instead of open embrasures. Hardwick Hall in Derbyshire, which is famous for its embroideries, is also known for the enormous number of its windows.

The expansion of trade at this time was bringing more money to the middle classes and bringing changes in their life style. The mistress of the great house, and the not so great, had servants to help her, and time for embroidery which every girl learnt from an early age. The maidservants also helped with the embroidery.

The link between more leisure and more wealth can be traced in countries other than Britain. In

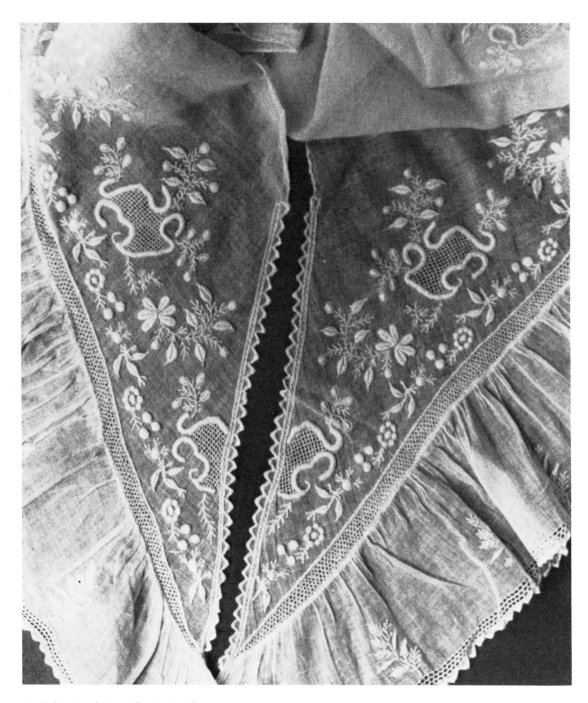

4   Fichu, Ayrshire work, nineteenth century
Edge of frill, insertion and motifs all contain drawn
diagonal ground
Embroiderers' Guild Collection, Melbourne

Denmark, where so many examples of the type of embroidery which we are discussing have been preserved, it is in the more productive and prosperous areas of the countryside that the finer and better examples of embroidery were made and used.

With the seventeenth century came taxes on the import of laces from France. In Denmark, Germany, the Low Countries and England the embroiderers produced great quantities of exquisitely embroidered fine, white muslin. The designs were closely allied to the lace designs and, in Germany, the work was called *Point de Dresde* and *Point de Saxe* and *Bohemian muslin lace*; in Denmark it was called *Tønder lace* and in Belgium it was known as *Flemish work* or *'work made in Dinant'*.

The aim was to contrast smooth areas made up of flat stitches with lacy areas where, with fine threads, the material was drawn into an endless variety of fine, open-work patterns.

The embroidery was used on kerchiefs (fichus), aprons, caps, cascading cuffs and petticoat flounces. It does not seem to have been used on baby's clothes, or rather, if it was, they wore out as these garments do not appear in existing collections.

We do not know whether it was used on domestic articles as, again, they do not survive. There are a few squares with sides of about 1 metre (1 yard) or slightly larger. One, attributed to Brussels manufacture, in the Industrie-und-Gewerbe-Museum at St Gall is very fine and embroidered with a wealth of flowers, foliage, lizards and a figure of a man. It would seem to be too fragile for general household use.

In the nineteenth century, a variety of this stitchery on muslin grew up in Scotland. Introduced to that country by an Italian named Luigi Ruffini, who learnt his trade in Dresden, it was principally done in the Ayrshire district. Here, it was an organised industry in conjunction with the manufacture of fine muslins in this area. The embroidery was done in their homes by women who were specialists in one particular stitch. Each did her section and then it was sent to someone else to do hers. The designs were mainly floral and so the work was known as 'Flowerin'. The drawn fabric stitches were chiefly used in the centres of the flowers. In later work the centres were cut out and filled with needle lace stitches and, in some, nets were placed behind the cut out areas. These nets looked very like the embroidered centres and a quick glance can be misleading. There is one piece in the Embroiderers' Guild Collection in Melbourne done in this way. Another piece of Ayrshire work in this collection has drawn diagonal ground used as a border and an insertion as well as in the design (4).

A similar type of work was also done in Ireland at that time. The wages paid were pitifully small by our standards and the children were also paid a pittance to keep the needles threaded so that no time was wasted.

It was from the tradition of work done in the peasant homes of Denmark that modern Danish drawn fabric patterns have come of the kind that we know today. Women working in their own homes have, over the years, simplified the elaborate designs of the eighteenth century and learned to work with more economical fabrics and threads.

Examples of drawn fabric embroideries in museums come from a very wide area. There is much from the Greek Islands and Italy done in the seventeenth and eighteenth centuries. There is a piece from Isfahan, Persia, in the Fitzwilliam Museum in Cambridge, dated seventeenth century.

In the eastern Mediterranean areas, coloured threads were used together with a wider range of stitches. In some of the work from this region, a number of metal threads were used. Stitches that we now think of as canvas work, were included in some Italian designs and the patterns bear striking resemblances to Assisi work. The only piece that I have seen attributed to Venetian make is in the collection of the National Gallery of Victoria in Melbourne. It is classified as seventeenth century, although it is completely different in design and stitch pattern from anything else that I have seen (5).

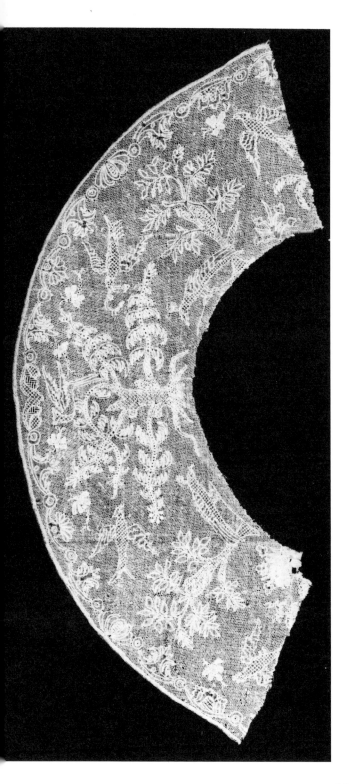

At some time, but just how early I have not been able to discover, embroidery on muslin, known as *Chikankari*, developed in India. This is done in cotton or silk on muslin using drawn fabric techniques, amongst others.

Today's use of drawn fabric prefers it to be monochromatic but still with emphasis on textural variety and differences in density of stitches.

This type of embroidery requires evenly woven fabrics, loose enough for the threads to be displaced by pulling them into bundles. This characteristic is to be found particularly in hand woven fabrics and probably accounts for the wide-spread use of this medium from the Copts to today.

Amongst the embroidered waistcoats of the eighteenth century are some of white linen and twill. Quilting and drawn fabric stitches french knots, satin stitch and stem stitch were all used in these elaborately ornamented garments.

Today, the articles embroidered are much the same (with the exception of the clothing styles, of course) although many look for attributes such as minimum care in their up-keep. The beauty of table linen, be it a large cloth or mats, worked in drawn fabric techniques, can never be disputed.

Large panels can be used as room dividers and bold pieces make effective wall hangings. Curtains offer wonderful opportunities for drawn fabric embroidery but in the hard, bright light of Australia one hesitates to put so much work on one's windows!

5   Portion of a collar, muslin lace, Italian, Venice, seventeenth century
The entire net-like background is drawn fabric. Trees, birds, insects are outlined in chain stitch with drawn fabric details
National Gallery of Victoria, Melbourne. Felton Bequest 1964 (1064.5)

White waistcoats

In the eighteenth century when men wore long waistcoats under full-skirted knee-length coats, some were made of white linen or twill and were beautifully embroidered with quilting, surface stitchery and drawn work.

For the quilting to be done, whether the Italian or the English variety, there needed to be two layers of material. Some writers say that in working these waistcoats the under layer was of a looser weave than the upper one and that in the areas to be drawn the surface was removed and the lower one then ornamented with open patterns.

During a visit to London in 1977 I had the opportunity of studying the four waistcoats in the possession of the Embroiderers Guild and the one at the Victoria and Albert Museum and in none of these is any material cut away. In one at the Guild some threads have been withdrawn in a small area and the material, thus made looser, has been drawn into patterns. In the Industrie-und-Gewerbe-Museum at St Gall in Switzerland there is also one done in this method, but the others in that collection have no material removed nor has the one in the Kunstindustriemuseet in Copenhagen.

As will be seen from the waistcoat in the Victoria and Albert Museum (6) and the waistcoat in the museum at St Gall (7), the design covers a large area and is worked closely. Not all the waistcoats have quilting – some were covered with surface stitchery. The variety of texture achieved is extremely interesting.

Embroidery in a similar manner to the waistcoat in the Victoria and Albert Museum is to be seen on the embroidered stomacher at St Gall. There is no quilting on either garment but drawn fabric embroidery is combined with surface stitchery in both (8).

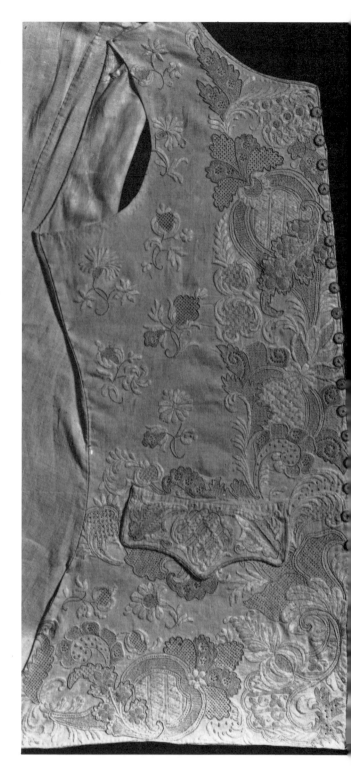

6   White linen waistcoat, eighteenth century
White linen with drawn fabric stitches, satin stitch and french knots. Buttons made from embroidered rings
Victoria and Albert Museum, London. Crown Copyright

19

7 Detail from a white waistcoat
Very fine quilting, french knots and four-sided stitch.
Some satin stitch
Industrie-und-Gewerbe-Museum, St Gall, Switzerland

8 Stomacher, detail
Drawn fabric stitches and surface stitchery are used in
this cream embroidery on cream linen
Industrie-und-Gewerbe-Museum, St Gall, Switzerland

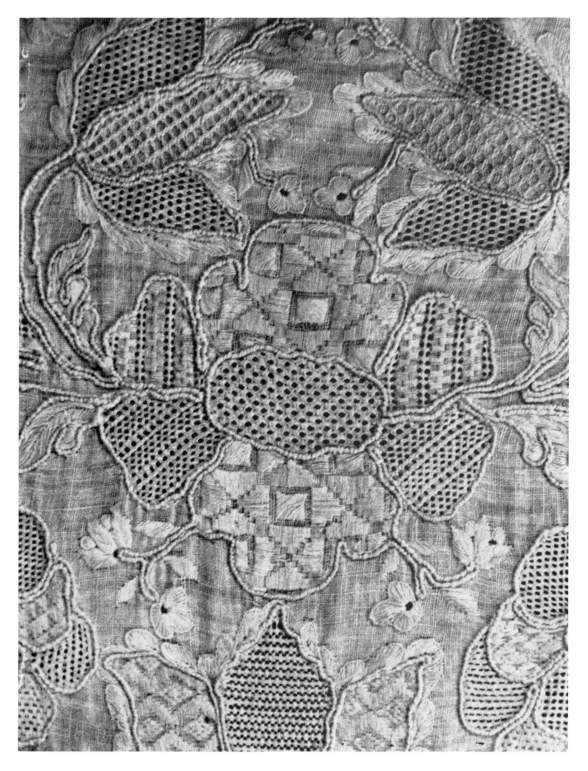

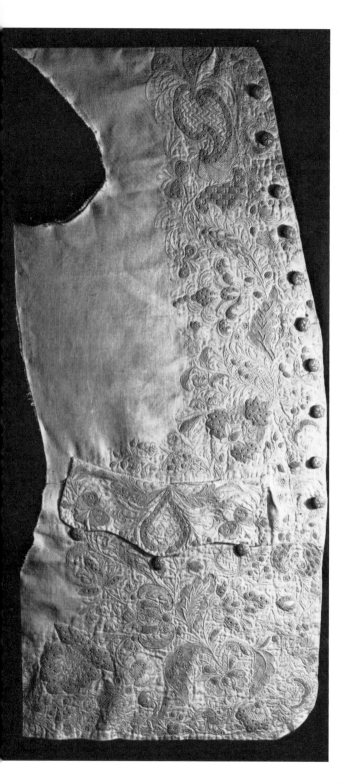

In one waistcoat at the Embroiderers' Guild, London, groups of french knots, in sixes like berries, are used to create background detail and the same groupings of french knots (but in larger numbers) are to be seen on the waistcoat in the collection at Copenhagen. This garment is of Norwegian origin (9).

One of the waistcoats at the Embroiderers' Guild has cotton twill for the upper layer and the mind boggles at the difficulty of 'drawing' or 'pulling' it into open work patterns.

Great use is made of fine, regular rows of crisp french knots for solid areas, sometimes with eyelets interspersed. A very sharp and strong edge, as outline, is achieved by couching fine cord with buttonhole stitch in a coarse thread and keeping the edge of the stitch on top of the cord. The two layers of material used in these waistcoats are both fairly fine so that the garments are not clumsy.

They are all so similar in style and so beautifully worked, that they were surely done by professionals. The sole example in London where the threads have been withdrawn, is by contrast, much coarser and the embroidery not so regular. There is also one at St Gall in a similar kind of embroidery but it is a different style. It is shorter, really only waist length, with turned-back lapels. It denotes a completely different fashion in clothes (10).

9   White twill waistcoat, Norwegian, eighteenth century
The charming buttons on this waistcoat have massed french knots with flower shaped plain areas in the centres. On the main part of the garment there are french knots, quilted details and drawn fabric fillings
Kunstindustrimuseet, Copenhagen
Photograph by Ole Woldebye

10   Short waistcoat, first half of eighteenth century
Cream twill with surface stitchery, some drawn fabric areas and french knots
Industrie-und-Gewerbe-Museum, St Gall, Switzerland

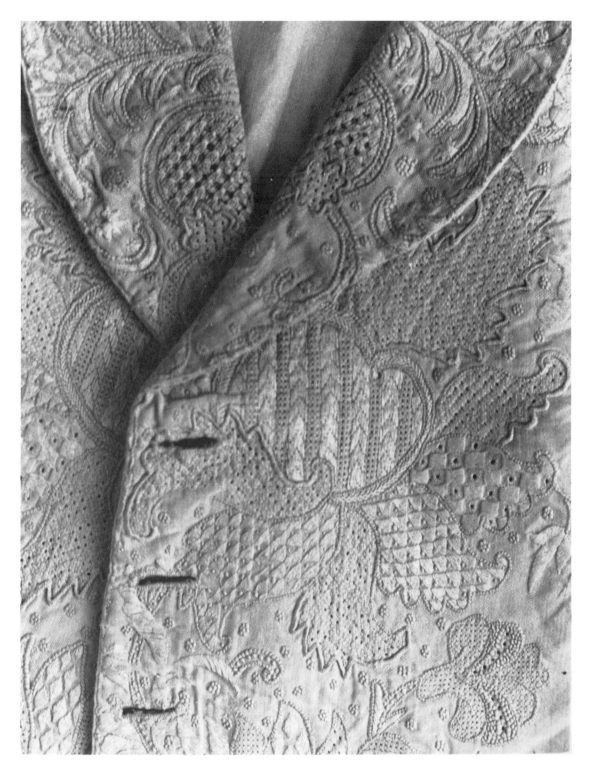

23

The high, raised outline in cord and buttonhole stitch is used on the Victoria and Albert waistcoat to outline the leaf in the lower left-hand corner and the leaf about level with the bottom of the armhole on the centre edge (6). The clustering of french knots in this garment is used as a filling stitch in some of the petals. This illustration repays examination using a magnifying glass. In fact, all the museum pieces illustrated deserve close study.

Occasionally the drawn work provides the background to the embroidery, not the design, as in the cream twill waistcoat that is in the Embroiderers' Guild collection.

Sometimes these quilted and embroidered waistcoats do not have any areas of drawn work. There were obviously various styles from which to choose.

The Art of Embroidery by Schuette and Müller-Christensen has an illustration of a beautiful christening robe in the same kind of embroidery. They call it *piqué* work and it has much drawn fabric embroidery amongst quilted outlines. One can see the similarity between the fine lines of quilting and piqué fabric. The example is noted as being in the Industrie-und-Gewerbe-Museum in Hamburg, Germany, and I regret that I have not seen it. There must be many places in Europe where there are good examples of this kind of embroidery.

Thérèse de Dillemont in her *Encyclopédie des Ouvrages de Dames* written early this century, describes piqué work such as this, but without the drawn fabric patterns and with surface stitchery. She says it was done in Italy in the fifteenth and sixteenth centuries.

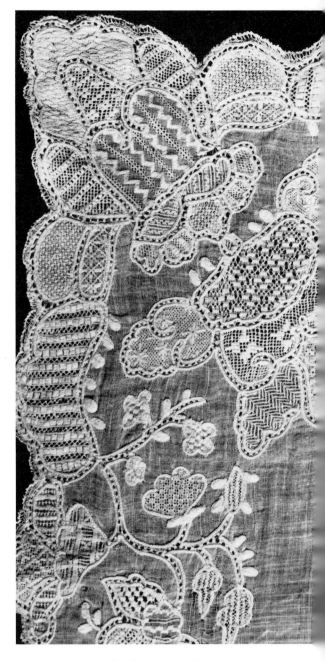

11   Apron, corner detail, seventeenth century
Drawn fabric fillings with chain stitch outlines.
Compare with illustration 5. Stitch patterns are much more complex in this example
Stranger's Hall Museum, Norwich
Photograph by Norfolk Museums Service

24

Eighteenth century aprons

This was a period when ladies considered an apron an integral part of their dress when at home. It was also a period when drawn fabric embroidery was popular and this combination of factors produced some exquisite examples.

Designs varied from simple sprigs scattered over the area, to plain aprons with elaborate corners and hems, and even some with scroll patterns all over the material. There are simple ones in costume displays at various museums throughout Europe. A good example of a piece of embroidery which has been an apron, now incomplete, is in the collection at the Stranger's Hall at Norwich which is part of the Norwich Castle Museum. This example has embroidered corners (*11*).

There are two complete aprons in the museum at St Gall. They are English, dating from the early eighteenth century. One has *Mary Winter, 1713* embroidered on it. Mary Winter's apron has a scroll design of flowers and leaves growing out of a mound, in the manner of crewel work designs. The other one has some of the 'fabulous' birds on it. The word 'fabulous' is used in notes on embroideries in the National Museum at Zurich. (This museum has some interesting, very old, white embroideries but none are drawn fabric.) These birds are unusual and distinctive in the embroideries of this period. The one on this apron is far better drawn than many and is really elegant (*12*).

There are 'fabulous' birds on a piece of embroidery in the Student's Room at the Victoria and Albert Museum. There is an almost identical piece in the collection at the Arts Centre at Melbourne. In both, the birds are quite unlike anything that ever flew. These birds bear a strong family resemblance to some of the Byzantine birds, found in the work from the Eastern Mediterranean embroideries in other mediums, though not in any drawn fabric designs that I have seen from that area.

12 *Fabulous Bird*, early eighteenth century
Although the bird doesn't contain drawn fabric stitches, much of the embroidery surrounding it does
Industrie-und-Gewerbe-Museum, St Gall, Switzerland

25

Muslin laces

Point de Dresde, Point de Saxe, Bohemian muslin
lace, Flemish Work or Tønder lace were names of
the very finest examples of drawn fabric embroidery ever done, and they were called 'lace' although
they were worked on fabric. They were made at a
time when high taxes were being levied against
importations of French laces. They bear striking
resemblance to the laces of the time. The patterns
must have been carried over from one medium to
the other.

The method of working was the same as in the
needle-made laces. To my delight, in the museum
at St Gall is an unfinished piece. It is a section for a
bonnet or a coif and the very fine linen is tacked
onto a firm parchment backing, as in making
needle-point lace, and the design, which would
have been drawn on the backing, has been transferred to the material with stem stitch outlining.
In this piece some of the background area had been
embroidered in an open filling stitch and the
design areas had not been started. A horrible stain
in one corner would suggest a reason why this
piece was never finished, but it tells a story to us
that would be untold, otherwise (13).

13   Unfinished bonnet. Point de Saxe
Design outlines in stem stitch before filling stitches
commenced
Industrie-und-Gewerbe-Museum, St Gall, Switzerland

27

The best of these examples are so fine that they are hard to tell from the traditional laces. In the museum at St Gall there are several strips that may have been bonnet ends, or lappets, as well as borders (14).

There is a superb piece in the same museum, a deep flounce dating from the second half of the eighteenth century. It is of French origin.

This type of embroidery was also used on handkerchiefs. An interesting example at St Gall has bobbin lace about 5 cm ($2\frac{1}{2}$ in.) wide and then a band of drawn thread work about 2.5 cm (1 in.) wide and then a beautifully embroidered corner including drawn fabric fillings. The transition from bobbin lace to embroidery is gracefully demonstrated in this example of French origin (see colour plate facing page 69).

The photograph of Tønder lace (15) is of an example in the Victoria and Albert Museum.

The example of Point de Dresde (16) is in the Kunstindustriemuseet in Copenhagen.

No matter what the scale of the embroidery the stitches used do not vary much from country to country and the vocabulary is quite large.

14   Muslin lace about 9 cm ($3\frac{1}{2}$ in.) wide
Design is unworked, outlined with a cordonnet, against a background of finest drawn stitches. These are used also in flower centres
Industrie-und-Gewerbe-Museum, St Gall, Switzerland

15   Fragment of Tønder lace
A superb example of its kind
Victoria and Albert Museum, London. Crown Copyright

29

16   Point de Dresde (Tyskland?), second half of the
eighteenth century
The whole area of this flounce is covered with a wide
variety of drawn fabric stitches. It is about 46 cm
(18 in.) wide and very, very fine
Kunstindustrimuseet, Copenhagen, Denmark
Photograph by Ole Woldebye

This is a beautiful small piece of Bohemian muslin lace in the National Gallery of Victoria collection, in the Arts Centre in Melbourne (*17*). In this piece, the density of the design area has been achieved by a layer of fabric placed underneath the top layer. The outline carries a *cordonnet* and the fine couching of this also holds the second layer in place. The second layer of material has been cut away where not needed.

A second piece in the same collection is classified as Tønder lace and uses the same method. It has open-petalled flowers that made me think of tiger lilies. It is quite narrow, about 5 cm (2½ in.) wide.

A third piece in this collection is also called muslin lace. It is Venetian, seventeenth century. This is quite different from any other piece I have seen. In the absence of more details, it is my guess that this is the earliest example I have seen. The design is outlined completely with chain stitch, with a few added eyelets and small groups of buttonhole stitches giving the effect of a beading. The whole background of this portion of a collar is drawn into a fine net-like pattern. The design is akin to other designs of this period and has a vaguely oriental feeling, with the tree which has affinities with crewel work of the same period.

17 Bohemian muslin lace, eighteenth century
The solid areas are emphasised with a second layer of fabric behind the surface. A cordonnet outlines the design and holds the second layer in place. The second layer is cut away elsewhere and fabric decorated with drawn fabric patterns
National Gallery of Victoria, Melbourne. Felton Bequest 1964 (1063.5)

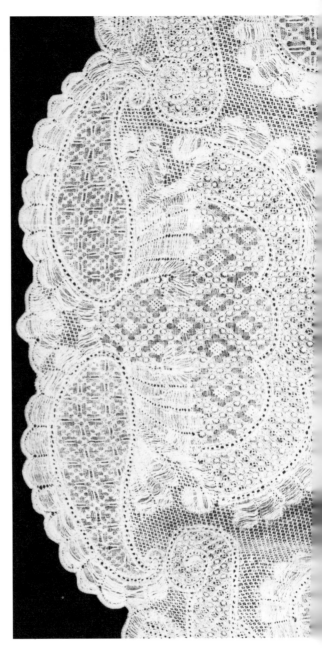

18(a) Engageante (one of a pair), Tønder lace, muslin work. Area photographed about 20 cm (8 in.). Danish eighteenth century
Right side showing double back stitch, chain and buttonhole stitches, and drawn fabric fillings
National Gallery of Victoria, Melbourne. Felton Bequest 1964 (1959 B5)

18(b) Engageante, Danish, eighteenth century
Wrong side showing long double back stitch which gives solidity to the design
National Gallery of Victoria, Melbourne. Felton Bequest 1964 (1059 B5)

19   Handkerchief, seventeenth century
Photograph by Norfolk Museums Service
This example has a large collection of drawn fabric
fillings. The embroidery has been retained from an
earlier article and applied to a later piece of fabric
Stranger's Hall Museum, Norwich

In the costume section of this same gallery, is a brocade gown with falling cuffs, known as *engageantes*, of Tønder lace. They are in perfect condition. The embroidery is on the finest linen, 90–95 threads = 2.5 cm (1 in.) and in the scrolling traditions of the lighter, more fragile examples. The denser areas are achieved with double-back stitch. Some of the longest threads cover quite a distance, up to 1 cm ($\frac{1}{2}$ in.). Although the design and the embroidery are of the highest quality in these cuffs, the pattern is not so conspicuous from a distance because of the closer weave of the fabric (*18 a and b*).

Delightful cuffs are to be seen on one exhibit at Platt Hall, Manchester.

Illustration (*19*) shows the corner of a handkerchief in the collection at Stranger's Hall, Norwich.

Eastern Mediterranean

Much embroidery in cut-work, drawn-fabric and drawn-thread work has been done and is still done, around the Mediterranean. The biggest difference from that worked in the tradition of the northern parts of Europe, is the use of colour in their work and their use of metal threads in this idiom.

In Turkey, the tradition of richness in their embroideries is carried through into their linen work. Many pieces incorporate the use of 'plate'. This metal thread, which is a fine, flat metal strip is extremely difficult to use in any way other than flat couching. But in Turkey they have used it widely in a needle and pulled it back and forth through the fabric. In many cases they sharpen the end of the metal strip and push it through the material, using pressure of the thumb to fold the strip. Later pressure is applied to the surface to flatten the stitches evenly. They have successfully mastered two problems; first, to pull it back and forth without splitting the material, and second, to keep it untwisted and lying flat. I have seen it oversewn on an edge, also as the edge of quite large eyelets and there is no twisting of the thread.

Today, they use flat lurex thread and it is very difficult to keep that untwisted. It is much more flexible than plate, which will break and crack if bent. As much Turkish work is reversible, the finishing has to be very carefully done. In the only piece I have been able to examine in detail, the end of the plate seemed to lie under one previous stitch only. Certainly, once the plate was in place it would not move like a flexible thread. When this book was almost complete, I chanced upon a piece of Turkish embroidery in a country town in Australia. It was a headscarf, a square of green cotton material similar to butter muslin with silver motifs worked in plate. The muslin was so flimsy that the stitches had pulled a very open pattern. It was impossible to tell which was the 'right' side when in use (stitch *27* page 126).

20   Eastern Mediterranean work
Embroidery in strong colour on a Drawn background
Victoria and Albert Museum, London
Crown Copyright

21   Eastern Mediterranean work
Skirt border in fine yellow silk and a small amount of
gold thread worked on white. Embroidery mainly in
open cross stitch
Embroiderers Guild Collection, Melbourne

Embroidery was frequently used on towel borders and on clothes of an earlier era. I saw one piece in a private collection, where a large triangular area of a square of pale orchid pink satin had been embroidered in silver plate in an all-over design using an openwork pattern. Although the piece had been worked by the owner's grandmother early this century, the owner had no idea how it had been done. It appeared to have been worked with a large needle and the design areas resembled punch work. I was told that this piece of embroidery would be used to hold the head scarf and night attire of a bride. A pink one would be for the bride and a blue one for the bridegroom. The square would be folded with the corners to the centre, like an envelope, and both would be placed between the sheets. A similar piece in blue satin is in the collection in the Topkapi Palace Museum in Istanbul.

The type of embroidery using plate as ordinary thread appeared on a gauzy, folded drape with large eyelets as part of a woman's costume in the Topkapi Museum.

Plate had also been used on a child's robe where the stitches made stripes about 2.5 cm (1 in.) wide that looked like gold braid.

There are beautiful embroidered towels with pulled work and gold embroidery, exhibited alongside a shaving robe of a sultan. The robe was cream silk with soft silk embroidery in a wide circular design around the neck.

It is hard to distinguish between embroideries in this part of the Mediterranean, there has been so much movement of population over the centuries that individual characteristics are uncommon. There are many examples to be seen of linen embroideries where the background is the drawn fabric with the pattern either left unworked or worked in quite dark shades of blue or red.

In his book *Mediterranean and Near Eastern Embroideries* (1935), A J B Wace has two illustrations where the pattern is worked in colour and the background is drawn. Illustration (*20*) is of an example in the Victoria and Albert Museum, London.

There is a very old piece in the museum at St Gall. It is Turkish and has bands of needle weaving and the embroidery is done in colour in open cross stitch.

Having seen an unfinished piece of linen work in the museum at St Gall, where one thread in four has been withdrawn both ways, it would seem that this method was possibly in general use. In that piece, the threads within the pattern areas do not seem to have been disturbed and it appeared that the edges had been delineated with an inconspicuous hem stitch. By contrast, one piece in the Benaki Museum in Athens looked as though the threads had been pulled out right across and then darned back within the design – there was an unevenness of weave appearing regularly in the solid areas. No doubt there were personal preferences amongst embroiderers, just as there are today.

The skirt border (*21*) is worked in open cross stitch in gold silk and some small amount of metal thread. It is in the Embroiderers' Guild Collection in Melbourne.

Persian

There is a hanging in the Fitzwilliam Museum, Cambridge, which is from Persia. It is seventeenth century from Isfahan. It is embroidered all over in a design of birds, animals and plants, in silk on a natural linen ground. The birds are in most beautiful shades of blue. The background is a regular square grid of pulled stitches.

In the National Gallery collection in Melbourne are two seventeenth century Persian embroideries. One is a table cover in natural linen, embroidered with tussore silk in an all over geometric pattern. Most of the work is cut and drawn but quite large triangular areas in all four corners, appear to be faggot stitch. The general feeling of the piece is of work done in diagonal lines. As it is mounted on dark red woollen material, it is impossible to see the back of the stitches.

The other piece is a linen head cover worked with dainty geometric motifs and this definitely has rows of faggot stitching in the working.

Chikankari or Chikan work

This embroidery originated in the Dacca area of India where muslins of the finest quality were produced. In *Handicrafts and Industrial Arts of India* (1960), Rustam J Mehta writes:

> The muslins of Dacca have rightly been famed for centuries and justly considered the masterpieces of the Indian weaver in cotton, for the extreme delicacy and the great beauty of the Dacca muslins of old, stand unsurpassed.

It is reported in this book that the Persian ambassador (1628–1641):

> on returning from India, presented to his master a muslin turban 30 yards in length, so exquisitely fine that it could scarcely be felt by the touch.

Other stories of the fineness of the muslins include the one of the princess upbraided by her father for appearing in public in a 'see through' sari (this occurred well over 100 years ago!) who asserted she had wrapped the sari around her body seven times. And another comment on night attire and underwear so fine that it wore out with a single wear. No wonder that embroideries on material such as this have not survived. Indians who have written of Chikan work speak in romantic similes.

Rustam J Mehta makes frequent mention of Mrs Kamala Dongerkery. Writing on the local significance of certain Indian embroideries in the *The Romance of Indian Embroideries* (1951), he quotes her as saying:

> The simple, yet beautiful, Chikankari of the Gangetic plains, too, must have its own message for the people, no doubt. Would it be wide of the mark if a suggestion was made that the purity of the waters of the holy rivers is reflected in Chikankari?

22 Bodice with Chikankari motif
Phanda knots, diagonal drawn ground and back stitch are used in this design
Embroiderers Guild Collection, Melbourne

While in *Masterpieces of Indian Textiles*, Rustam J Mehta, writes:

> An extremely lovely and elegant style of embroidery is the Chikan work of Lucknow but also produced in Calcutta, Dacca, Varanasi, Bhopal, Allahabad and Gaya. Done in white on cotton, linen or silk, it is aesthetically rich though without colour and is distinguished by elegant simplicity and chaste purity. Here is no flamboyance but the quiet dignity of refined aesthetic values – like moonlit beauty dimly seen through a veil.
>
> The best Chikan embroidery comes from Lucknow where is produced work of great beauty and remarkable distinction. It is believed that the craft really originated in Bengal and was taken to Lucknow during the reigns of the luxury-loving Nawabs of Oudh. In Lucknow Chikan work, off-white or yellowish Tusser (Tussore) silk from the wild Indian silkworm is used, unlike that from other places and this forms a point of distinction. The superb embroidery of floral designs is best when done on the finest of muslins, the production of which was an old industry in Lucknow.

Mehta also reports that a Dr James Taylor recorded:

> A skein (of cotton) which a native measured in my presence, in 1846, and which was carefully weighed afterwards, proved to be in the proportion of 250 miles to the pound.

References by English writers on Chikan work do not seem to be easily come by, but in *The Embroidress* No 50 (1934), Mrs K M Harris, who for some time was editor of this magazine, writes:

> Chikan work . . . is an artistic and delicate form of what might be called a purely indigenous needlework of India.

She mentions that Phanda is the most attractive type of stitch. Phanda is the millet seed and gives its name to a knotted stitch, the presence of which is the surest sign of high class work. She gives an open grounding stitch which is used, not the well-known Indian drawn ground. It is row upon row of double stitch, which must not be confused with double back stitch. Chikan uses double stitch on the thread or not. (Both these Indian stitches are included in the chapter *Stitches and how to make them*.)

23 Chikankari band, 5 cm (2 in.) wide
The stitches used are phanda knots, diagonal drawn ground and back
Embroiderers Guild Collection, Melbourne

40

Mrs Harris points out that the Chikandoz – the name frequently given to the professional male embroiderer – works by putting his needle into the material in the opposite direction from common usage in Europe. That is, he pulls his stitch away from him.

An article by W G Raffé, ARCA on the 'Embroideries of India', in *The Embroidress* No 72 (1939), contains some additional information.

> This work is done almost entirely by men, Moslem professionals, working for handcraft firms who run the trade. They employ boys from 10 up to men of 60.
>
> These firms possess huge numbers of incised wooden blocks very similar to those used for cotton printing in colours. These blocks are used to print a light washable grease on muslin, by one man whose special job it is. Then the embroiderers set to work sitting cross-legged on a *durrie*, usually they are engaged in piece work. The frame is not much used.
>
> The articles made were confined once to objects for Indian use . . . fine tray cloths, the sari and choga and the popular pie-shaped cap favoured for Moslem use, but now known (undecorated) as the *Ghandi* cap. Now many articles are made for European use . . .
>
> The stitches are few, simple and rapidly made. For the commoner work, *tapichi*, a darning stitch is used. Another effective stitch is *bhukia*, a double back-stitch . . . Another similar effect is achieved by a tiny appliqué, named *khatao*, while boys begin work in designs that require many hundreds of French knots or tiny satin stitch. Skilled men use *jali*, making a trellis pattern by button-holing around threads pulled together not unlike Hedebo. Most Chikan work is done with fine white cotton but sometimes a fine-spun tussore silk is used.

The satin stitches are built up on top of each other and the stitch is called Murri – the word for the rice grain. Overall the satin stitch clusters may measure no more than 1.5 mm ($\frac{1}{16}$ in.).

The most recent reference to Chikan work is by Irwin and Hall in their publication *Indian Embroideries* (1973). They say:

> The pattern may be worked in stitchery upon the surface of the fabric in open work or in shadow work. Sometimes several of these techniques are combined in the same pattern.

People to whom I have spoken, who lived in India during the twentieth century, are all of the impression that this kind of embroidery grew up during the nineteenth century under British influence but this does not seem to have been the case.

In 1881 Mrs F B Palliser wrote a *Descriptive Catalogue of the lace and embroideries in the South Kensington Museum*. In it she says that the embroidered laces of Denmark in the eighteenth century were commonly called 'Indian Work'.

There is an illustration in Irwin and Hall's book of a handkerchief embroidered all over. There is a large flower in the centre and the design moves outwards with geometric precision in flowers and foliage. They also have photographs of small borders suitable for bands at neck and edges of robes.

The Embroiderers' Guild in Melbourne have a bodice and a small piece of a band and some handkerchiefs (*22 and 23*). The bodice has drawn fabric work included in the design, as well as Phanda knots. The band has many Phanda knots and also drawn work. It was the presence of these pieces in this collection which prompted me to pursue this part of the subject in such detail.

I have been told by friends who lived in India, that the name means, literally, 'shiny work'. This could certainly apply to the work done in silk on muslin and to some contemporary work I have seen, which was done by machine in a shiny rayon thread.

Samplers

In the Victoria and Albert Museum, London, there is a Swiss sampler of drawn fabric stitches. However, this does not seem to have been a favourite form of embroidery in that country and today it is not considered typical of Swiss embroidery (*24*).

I had the opportunity of studying a beautiful sampler in a private collection in Copenhagen, dated 1818. It contained 38 different stitches. All of them can be found in text books today but the computations of combining drawn satin stitch and others make the possibilities seem endless (see colour plate facing page 44).

There was another sampler in this same collection, the linen was finer and an area in the centre had a lace border reproduced. There was no date.

Samplers of purely drawn stitches do not seem to have survived in such great numbers as have some others. Of those that have, most are divided into areas about 7 cm (2–3 in.) square with perhaps, a central motif. Illustration (*25*) is on white linen, 48–50 threads = 2.5 cm (1 in.), and it is mounted over pink linen.

Samplers can be purely stitch vocabularies or they can be quite imaginative. Older ones tend to be very precise, though the Danish one illustrated is quite decorative.

I have included a couple of contemporary ones by way of contrast (*26 and 27*). Another one is stitches that I have found in old samplers, which are combinations of well-known stitches. These are in columns 2, 3 and 4. Column 1 is diagonal drawn ground used in two different ways, squared ground stitch and double faggot stitch (each stitch is done twice) (*28*).

24   Small mat, 15 cm (6 in.) square
Pattern made up of pulled satin stitch
Purchased Heimatwerk, Zurich, Switzerland

25   Detail of Danish sampler dated 1818
Private Collection, Copenhagen, Denmark
See colour plate overleaf

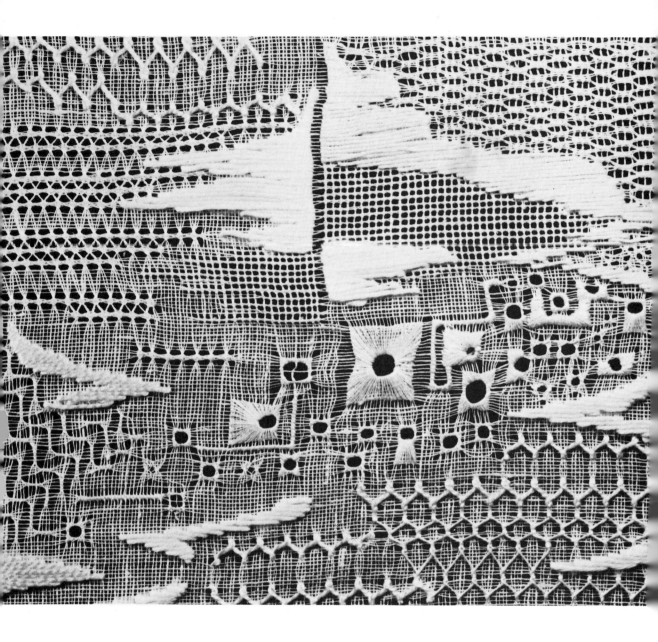

26   Contemporary sampler
Stitches included are honeycomb, alternating four-
sided, four-sided, Finnish, satin, step and eyelets
Photograph by Mary-Ellen Belville

Sampler 1818
Private Collection
Copenhagen

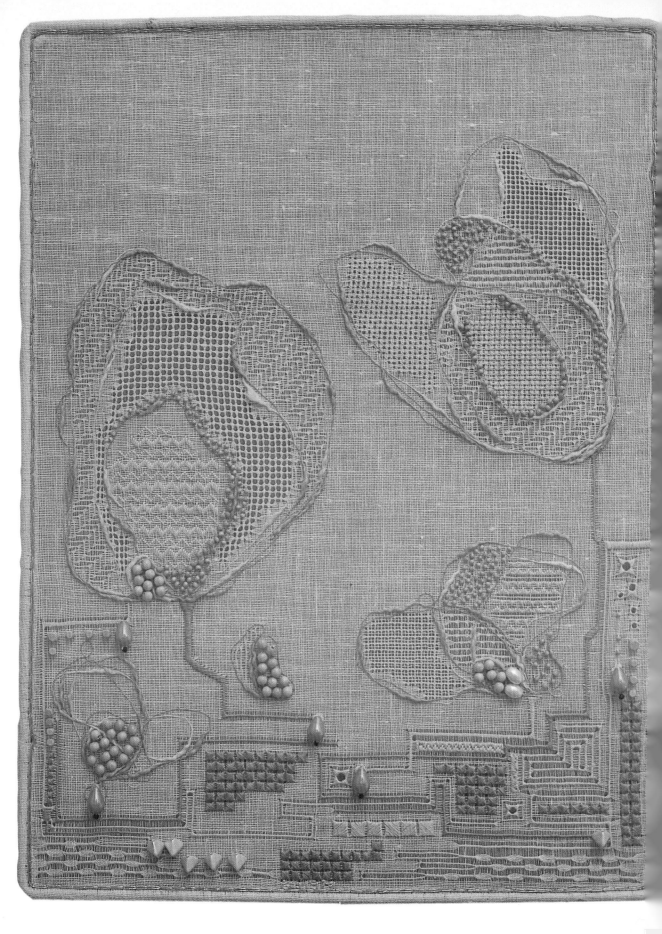

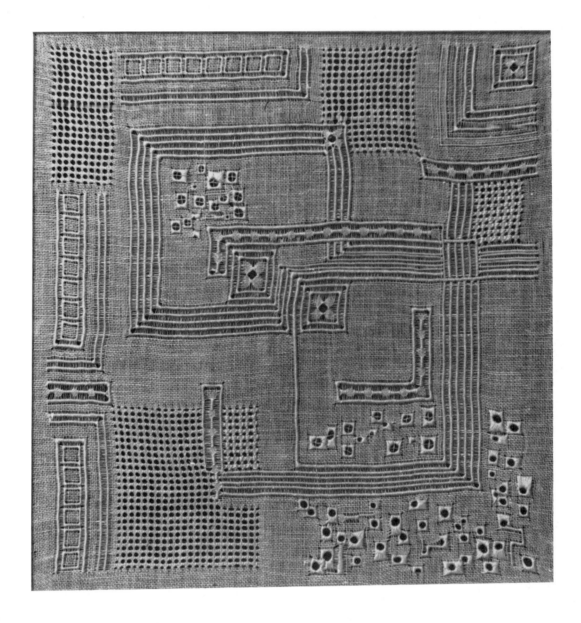

27 Contemporary sampler
Stitches used are pulled satin stitch and eyelets with
four-sided stitch

Colour plate facing
Flower shapes
by Edna Wark

45

28   Collection of traditional stitches

Ecclesiastical embroidery

Although this kind of embroidery is not the traditional way of doing ecclesiastical cloths there is no reason why it cannot be used for this purpose.

The designs can either be positive or negative and crosses of all shapes and sizes can be worked without trouble on the grain of the fabric.

Beryl Dean has included drawn fabric stitches amongst other techniques in her panel *The Annunciation*. The centres of the lilies and the decoration on the dress, are drawn fabric work. The shadow beside the figure is indicated with eyelets. The hand-woven linen and lurex fabric was very sympathetic to this method of working (*29*).

29　*The Annunciation*　2.4 m × 1.2 m (8 ft × 4 ft)
Beryl Dean, London
One of a set of five panels commissioned by the
Friends of St George's Chapel, Windsor
Photograph by Millar and Harris, London

47

Experimenting with techniques

Earlier reading had led me to believe that eighteenth-century embroiderers had, in some cases, worked on a double layer of material and that they had cut away surface areas and then worked drawn fabric patterns on the lower layer of more loosely woven fabric. As a variety of examples were not available for study in Australia, I decided to look at the method for myself.

In Illustration (*30*) I worked a sample with the upper layer of Old Bleach linen and the lower layer of coarse scrim. 20 threads = 2.5 cm (1 in.).

I found the result satisfying and decided to embroider a cloth, for the top of a chest of drawers, in two layers of Evenweave linen. The top layer was 27 threads = 2.5 cm (1 in.) and the lower 35 = 2.5 cm (1 in.). The result is not so pleasing as there is insufficient contrast in the density of the two materials (*31*). The design bore resemblance to the design on the metal fittings of the chest.

The method used was to tack carefully both layers of material together throughout the entire area. The design was transferred by tacking through a paper with the design on it. After tacking, the paper was torn away.

The outline was worked in a double row of pin stitch (which incidentally, looks like spoke-stitching done by a machine).

Then the upper layer was cut away very carefully within the design areas and drawn fabric stitches worked. (Lace scissors proved a boon for the cutting process.)

When all areas were worked, a row of raised chain band was worked as outline so that any rough edges of linen were completely covered.

Finally, all excess linen was cut away from behind the main body of the cloth and the edge worked.

30   Experimental exercise on two layers of fabric – Old Bleach linen and loose scrim

31 Experimental exercise worked on two layers of
evenweave linen. Stitches used are ringed four-sided,
step, Finnish, pebble and raised chain band
Photograph by Mary-Ellen Belville

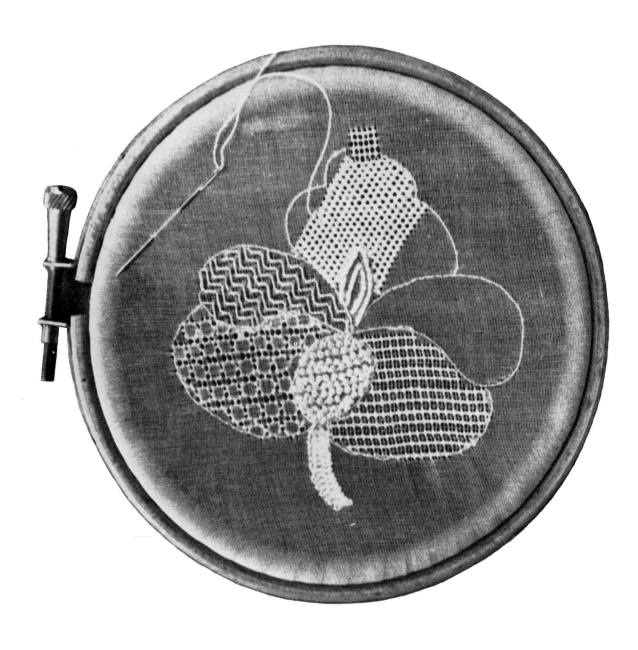

32 Experimental exercise worked on organdie
72 threads = 2.5 cm (1 in.)
Embroidery hoop = 11.5 cm (4½ in.)
Stitches used are step, ringed four-sided, ringed back,
four-sided and Mürver

50

While studying historic pieces in Europe I was amazed at the fineness of the materials that had been used.

The Danish sampler (25) I estimated at 48–50 threads = 2.5 cm (1 in.) but many specimens were much finer than this. Unfortunately, they were in glass cases and I could only guess. But I did try a small piece of embroidery on the finest piece of cotton material that I could find (32).

It is certainly not nearly as fine as the work I saw. It was worked on organdie which is 72 threads = 2.5 cm (1 in.). It was an exhausting exercise in concentration!

Having seen the unfinished bonnet at St Gall, I sewed a piece of Evenweave linen (33a) onto a piece of strong brown paper, on which the outline of the design was drawn in bold, black ink.

The outline was worked in pearl cotton no 12 in stem stitch and then the design filled in with drawn fabric stitches using DMC Broder no 50.

The outlines were then accentuated by whipping the stem stitch with pearl cotton no 3.

The work was then removed from the paper. The veins were added – being fine cords made from pearl cotton no 3 (33b).

The piece was then ready for finishing. I felt that as the whole thing was a bit of nostalgia, it would be best made into a dainty cushion, so a straight strip of linen – twice as long as the circumference of the cushion – was worked with danish picot edge and a row of blocks to match the background. It was then gathered and inserted between the two pieces of the cushion.

I found this method a very satisfactory way of working. The needle slipped easily between linen and paper. It meant that beginning and ending of threads had to be done inconspicuously on the surface but that was not really a problem. I pulled the coarse pearl cotton through to the back of the paper and finished the ends when the linen was removed from the paper (33c).

The piece of work was about 35.5 cm (14 in.) square and anything larger would be a bit cumbersome to handle mounted on paper. On a tablecloth, for instance, the area under attention could be done in this way, then another and so on. I would still use a frame for experimental work requiring great tension in the stitches.

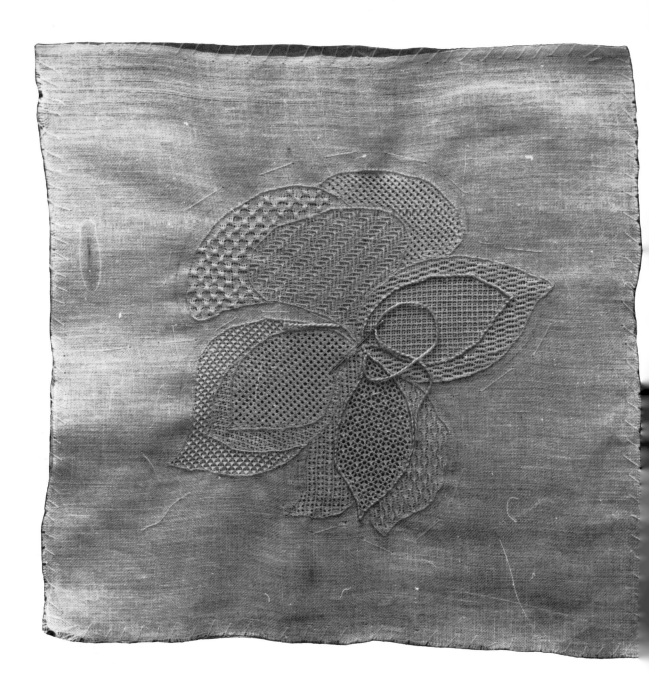

33 Experimental exercise
(a) Work tacked onto firm brown paper in progress

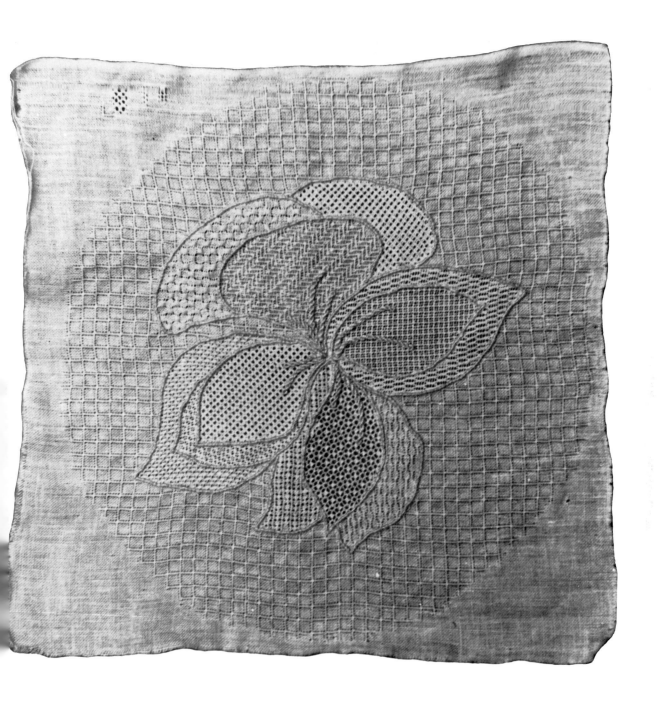

(b) Work completed and removed from paper

(c) Finished work

54

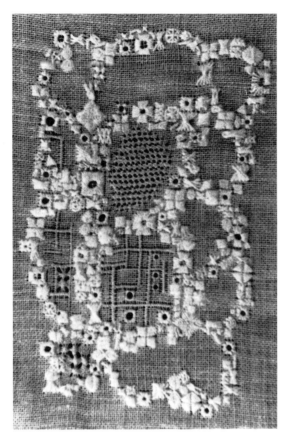

34 Experimental exercise
Jean Lange, Adelaide, South Australia
One quarter of the central design for a cloth. Wide
variety of threads with different finishes were used
for the solid areas.

35 Experimental exercise
Thyra Robertson, Perth, Western Australia
Very open effect achieved only by tension. No threads
have been withdrawn. Interesting texture has been
achieved by a variety of stitches

Illustration (34) is of a trial piece for the centre of a
table-cloth. Jean Lange, Adelaide, intends it to be
one quarter of the design and to place it in the
centre so that it will show to advantage and not be
uneven where plates will be set.

In this experimental piece Thyra Robertson, Perth,
has achieved a very open design purely by pulling
and drawing her threads apart. No threads have
been withdrawn. She has, also, created some
attractive texture. It would make a lovely box top.
Deep gold fabric has been placed behind the top
layer which is cream with cream embroidery (35).

Planning drawn fabric embroideries

Requirements for this kind of embroidery are:
1   Material where the threads can be readily displaced by being drawn together in bundles.
2   An assortment of threads.
3   Blunt or ball-pointed needles.
For strictly traditional work you need thread equal in weight to the individual threads in your fabric; for good measure both a tightly twisted one, such as Pearl cotton and a smoother one, such as Broder; for coarse work there is a really matt one, such as Anchor Soft or DMC Rétors a Broder to give good contrast, and the needle should have an eye that will comfortably hold the thread.

I prefer a needle with a round eye for all types of embroidery, although an egg-shaped one, as in a crewel or tapestry needle, is more generally liked. I think a round eye does not chafe the thread so much but the only round eyed needle with a blunt point is a ball-point.

For creative work a variety of threads is needed and necessarily, an assortment of needles. The correct size of needle will make a hole large enough to allow the needle with the thread to pass through the fabric easily and yet, the eye must just hold the thread comfortably. Nothing is more exasperating than for the thread to slip out of the needle continually because the eye is too big, but against this, I am convinced that a coarse needle which pushes the threads apart, so that the displacement is not entirely by the tension on the working thread, is less likely to cause puckering.

Embroidery on dress

Embroidery of this kind presents its own special problems.

When a girl had one special garment that was her wedding dress and her best dress for the rest of her life, more or less, she was expected to put in the time and effort to make it elaborate and gorgeous, as was the case in the beautiful garments that were part of the folk tradition of earlier centuries. In many cases she was also expected to have made and embroidered a number of shirts for her husband! But, with the ever-changing fashions of the present day, the scope for beautifully embroidered garments is somewhat limited.

Borders and motifs of drawn fabric stitches can be used on loosely woven cottons and on linens. Some evenly woven woollen dress materials also lend themselves to this type of embroidery. Cheesecloth, which should be easy to work, had disappointed me when I've used it, the stitch patterns were lost in the crêpe fabric.

Delightful summer handbags can be made of linens and furnishing fabrics in styles formal or informal (36).

A shawl of light-weight wool, with scattered free form flowers in open work, could be light and lovely. They could be worked in fine gold or silver lurex.

The embroidery is easier to do in designs going vertically from shoulder to hem, and around sleeves, or as a bib, than around the hem-line of the caftan-type gown that is so popular today. This is because the hem-line is slightly curved and the drawn fabric embroidery is done on the grain of the material. However, on a simple straight skirt, no matter what length, a horizontal band would be no trouble to do. The popular wrap-around skirt could be embroidered down the straight front edge.

Just a couple of over-lapping circles on the side of the bodice can give interest to an otherwise simple woollen frock – or a motif on a blouse sleeve.

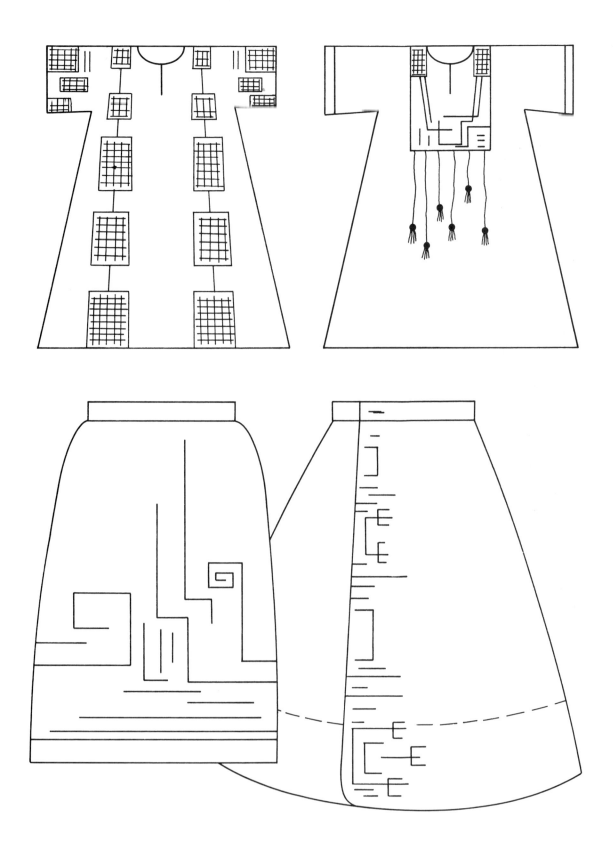

36 Handbag
Melba Ashby, Mt Gambier, South Australia
Four-sided, ringed four-sided and satin stitch have
been used

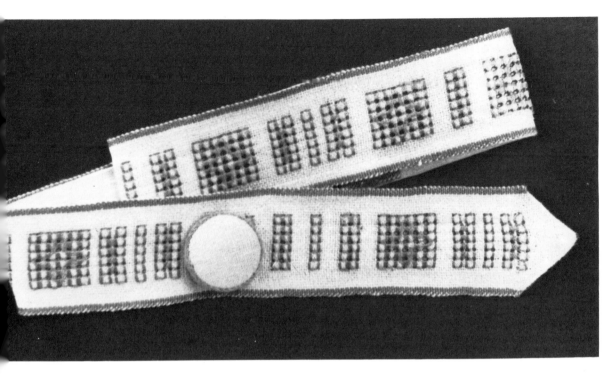

37 Belt Four-sided stitch forms the pattern with
some superimposed colour

Belts

Effective belts can be made using the linen strip
with a narrow edge of colour, often used for
making carriers for trays.

A simple arrangement of lines and blocks is all
that is needed. Groups of eyelets may be included.
For fastening add a buckle or a large button
covered in matching linen. It can have a line of
raised stem band or several close rows of stem
stitch in the same colour as the edge embroidered
on the rim of the button. The belt can be stiffened
or not as desired (37).

Things to make

There are many small things to be made which will be appreciated as your individual touch is recognised. They will be welcome as gifts or for any fair or bazaar.

Boxes

The lids or sides of small boxes can be decorated with drawn fabric embroidery. The one illustrated has used the bottom of a Camembert cheese tin! When the lid is removed, wash the tin thoroughly. For a little padding under the linen, use a layer of felt. Cut the necessary shapes in felt and lace the edges together with tiny stitches, so that there will be no ridges.

You will need to cut cardboard to match the size of the tin for a lid. The strip around the side, on the outside, is on the straight grain of the material and may be embroidered. For a really good finish inside, cut the strip on the bias so that you can stretch it to curve nicely on the rim. There must be no fullness (*38*).

A little embroidery on the lining in the base is attractive. A layer of padding between lining and cardboard in the base and under the lid gives a pleasing appearance.

There are well-made small wooden boxes in several shapes and sizes with recessed lids into which a piece of embroidery, mounted over a piece of cardboard, can be stuck.

38   Small box, diameter 9 cm (3½ in.)
The stitches on cream and natural linen are four-sided,
ringed four-sided, step stitch and Mürver
Photograph by Mary-Ellen Belville

Bookmarkers

Any scraps of even-weave material can be used for these. The size is optional. Add an elegant tassle (*39*).

Needle book

This one is a straight strip. The size should fold comfortably into three (see line drawing).

Hem the edge of the material with danish picot stitch and embroider one-third of the length at one end. Cut 2 or 3 pieces of flannel to fit and attach down the centre of the flannel to the linen. The edges of the flannel can either be buttonholed or left raw if cut with pinking shears.

Now, fold the strip into three. Add fastenings if desired (*39*).

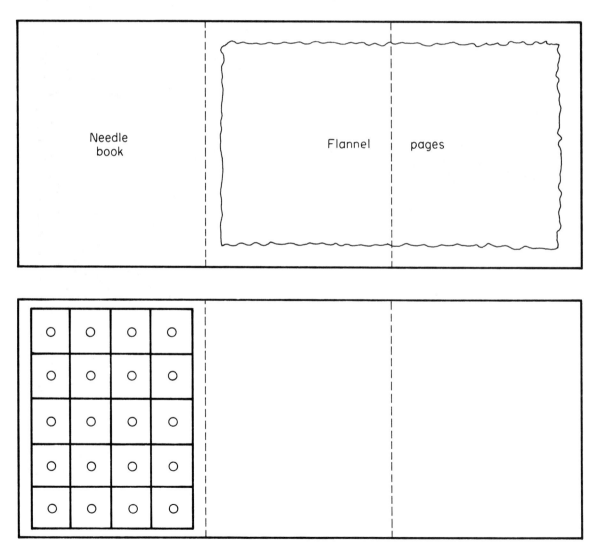

39   Needle-book and bookmark
Muriel Thorn, Melbourne

Pincushion

Cut a piece of linen 21.5 × 14 cm (8½ × 5½ in.). Overcast the edges. Mark the centre with a line of stitches. Make sure you follow the same thread all the way.

Mark with stitches all the lines on the line drawing indicating top, bottom and sides. Count the threads to make sure that they match (see line drawing on facing page).

Buttonhole over 2 threads, and leave 2 threads between each stitch along all tacked lines. (Where there are two lines shown, make sure the buttonhole stitches are back to back.)

Making sure it is in the centre, do some embroidery in the middle of the square marked top and in the corners.

Do some embroidery on the 4 sides. Count your threads to be sure whether the stitch you have in mind will fit evenly into the area available.

When the embroidery is completed press on the wrong side and cut away surplus material as shown by wavy lines and shaded areas.

With the same thread as used for buttonholing oversew the corners by catching the edges of your buttonhole stitches together. Push the extra material to the inside.

Fold the square marked bottom so that it meets the sides of the top thus making the box shaped pin cushion.

Sew along the sides leaving one side partially open so that you can insert the stuffing. Be sure to stuff your pin cushion very firmly as this is what holds it in shape. Also, be sure to push the filling right into the corners so that it is trim and smart. Complete sewing up.

Pincushions made this way will go through the washing machine and come up smiling. For filling – use Dacron filling (*39*).

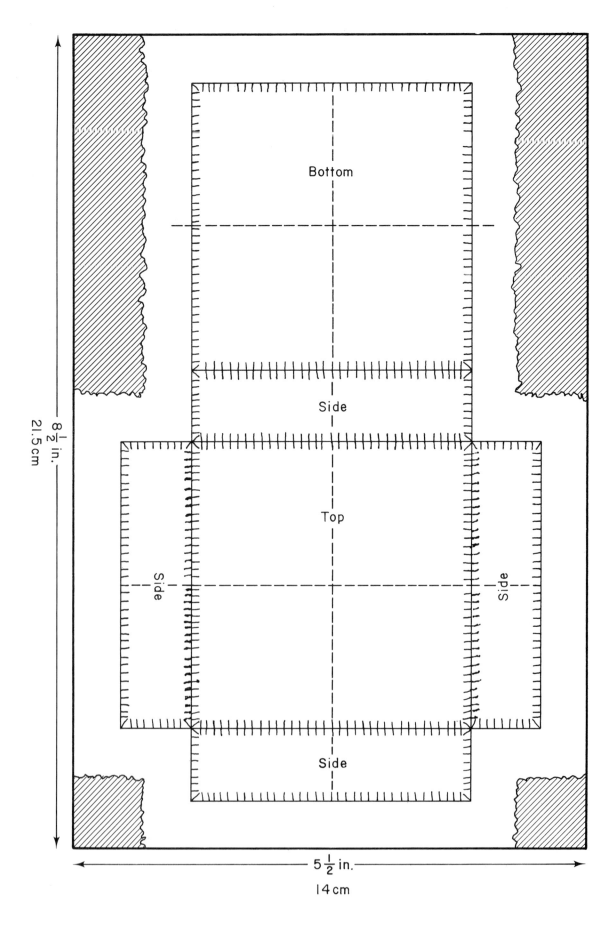

Bottom

Side

Top

Side

Side

Side

$8\frac{1}{2}$ in.

21.5 cm

$5\frac{1}{2}$ in.

14 cm

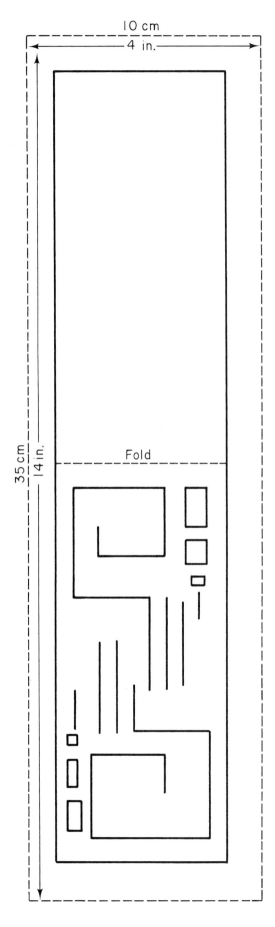

Spectacle case

Some people like their spectacles to be protected by a case with a firm interlining. Some like theirs to be soft with a smooth, silky lining that will not scratch the lenses.

For this kind you need only a straight strip of linen – for serviceability – coloured rather than white.

Geometric patterns are quite suitable.

The size of the piece of material needed depends on the size of the spectacles – 35 × 10 cm (14 × 4 in.) is usually quite large enough (see line drawing). Sunglasses are frequently larger than ordinary spectacles.

If you are making a gift for an embroiderer friend who wears 'look-overs', your case can be very small and dainty.

When the design has been worked do the first row of danish picot edge 7 mm ($\frac{1}{4}$ in.) from the edge, all around. Then fold the strip in half, so that you have a tube which is closed at the bottom.

Join the sides with 2 buttonhole stitches between each picot. Slide the needle between the two layers so that the thread does not show between the stitches. Use a thread that matches the fabric.

Work the second row of the danish picot edge around the top.

Make the lining to fit using a silky material with an interlining of dacron wadding. Place inside the tube and slip stitch into place (*40*).

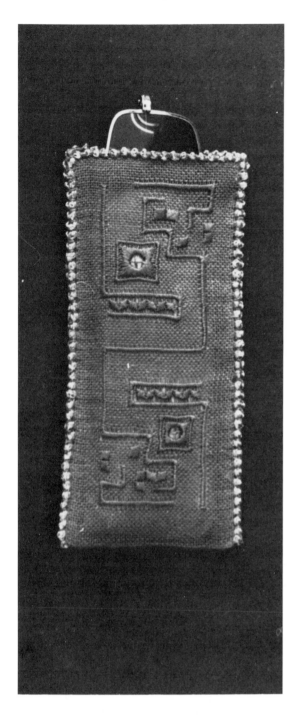

40   Spectacle case
Danish picot edge in lurex, design in pulled satin
stitch, eyelets and satin stitch blocks

67

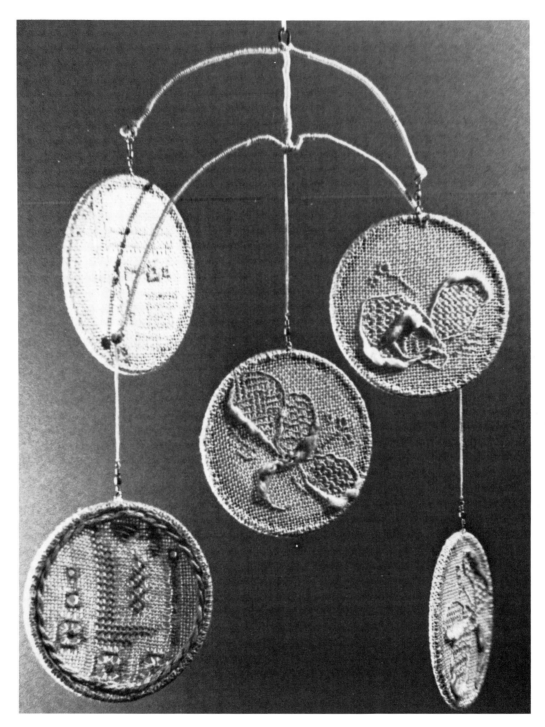

41   Mobile by Mary-Ellen Belville, Geelong, Australia
Photograph by Mary-Ellen Belville

Corner of handkerchief showing bobbin-lace border, drawn thread
inner border and finely embroidered corner containing drawn fabric work

IndustrieundGewerbermuseum, St Gall, Switzerland

Mobiles

These units were made over cheap metal bracelets obtained from a chain store. If you can get it, piano wire is strong and satisfactory for the cross pieces but these were made with florist's wire (41).

Lampshade

These can be made any size to suit the base. Use a drum shaped wire frame. It is a good idea to mount the material on the frame before doing the embroidery. You are in no doubt as to where you need the pattern to be and you can arrange some of your decoration to cover the seam. It is not quite so easy as working on an embroidery frame but it has the same effect of keeping the tension of the stitches at the correct level. Be sure to mark the grain of the fabric with a line of coloured thread near the top and bottom edges before mounting on the frame so that you will be sure the grain is parallel to the edge — otherwise a border stitch can wander disastrously.

Stretch the fabric firmly over the frame and sew into place. After your embroidery is finished you can spray it gently with water and leave to dry. The material should shrink just sufficiently to make the fabric as good a fit as it is possible to get.

If desired, line your finished embroidery with a fine soft silk and bind your edges in any way you wish — with velvet or silk or braid. The finish would be as simple as possible so as not to detract from the embroidery (see line drawing).

Colour plate facing
Detail of flounce
French *c* 1700
Industrie-und-Gewerbe-Museum, St Gall, Switzerland

69

Designing

If you are diffident about trying to design for yourself, forget the word 'design'. A design is merely a 'plan to fill a space'. 'Simple' is the most important word in this context. The best designs are simple. They have impact which is all too often lost in a wealth of unnecessary detail. Anyone who arranges flowers, decorates a cake or makes an attractive bowl of salad, creates a design!

To begin with consider the purpose of your embroidery . . . A table mat or tablecloth will need to be smooth so that the plates will rest flat. So, will you put the design around the edge, or will it be at one end, or all over?

The pattern must match the scale of the article. Geometric patterns, in drawn fabric stitches always look well on table linen.

Try a single flower on a stem with maybe a leaf or two, freely drawn for preference. Remember, contemporary thinking does not aim to reproduce every detail photographically – it is content to create an impression. This is nothing new. They have been doing it in China and Japan for centuries.

A slubbed thread gives a beautifully free outline (see colour plate facing page 45).

You may prefer to get your shape by playing around with dropping your outline thread onto the material. This method has the advantage that you can move it, or even take it off, as many times as you need. When you have a shape that pleases you, pin the thread in place wherever it crosses – elsewhere, if needed – and slip stitch it into place as invisibly as you can.

You can plan geometric patterns either on graph paper or by cutting shapes in paper and moving them about on your fabric. When you get a pleasing arrangement pin them in place and then tack around them in a coloured thread. Or you can trace their pattern and then set the tracing paper in place and tack through the lines using coloured cotton. Make a very small stitch on top and a larger one underneath and then the tracing will lift off quite easily without tearing. You may want to refer to it while working. Do not use a very dark cotton for tacking as it can leave a mark when eventually you pull it out.

In making a design, let some shapes overlap and leave unequal spaces between the various shapes. A pattern that has no variation of shapes can become boring, but some unity of shapes is desirable.

If you have a photograph or an illustration which you wish to use as the basis of your design, cover it with tracing paper – non-waxed lunch wrap (greaseproof paper) is quite satisfactory – and just trace the outline. This simplifies it and makes you aware of the shapes only.

When you have planned the basic shapes of your design, start thinking about the stitches you will use. Play off different textures against each other, have solid areas against very lacy ones, leave unworked areas to complement your worked areas, include knotted stitches. Do not give every shape a hard outline. Perhaps accent one side only with a definite outline. Consider massing eyelets together . . .

If you are planning a wall-hanging, a room-divider or a curtain you can be far more venturesome with your stitchery. Your designing will be on a bolder scale but the same rules apply.

Think carefully about the balance of your design. It need not, necessarily, be symmetrical.

It must have solidity at the bottom to grow from. A triangular motif – not necessarily an equilateral one – is usually pleasing.

Try not to have a line that cuts your design in half, be it horizontally, vertically or diagonally, 1:3–2:3 is much better.

Do not place your design so low that it looks as if it is falling out the bottom of the material – or so high that it looks as if it is taking off into outer space.

Do not be tentative. Be bold and have the courage of your convictions. After all, YOUR design should express your ideas. Before you commence DO make sure that you have plenty of material around the edges. Nothing is more frustrating than to discover, after you have begun that another inch all around would have made it so much easier to do the finishings. I have seen panels that look as if the design has no room to breathe.

This is one area where it is imperative to have a clear picture in your mind as to what is achieved by colour and what by stitch.

There are plenty of other areas where variety of colour can be exploited. Let us enjoy the beauty of variety in density and texture in this connection.

To sum up:
1   Consider scale – the proportion of the design to the background area.
2   Evaluate tone and density of stitch patterns.
3   Do be sure that the balance of the design is pleasing, ie that some areas within the design do not completely out-weigh others, but remembering that variety is needed in the shapes and sizes of the parts that make up the whole.

If you are planning a panel as a room divider or wish to hang it on a glass screen, you have a special problem. It must look good from both sides. This will affect your choice of stitch and place special demands on the finishing of your stitches. In many cases it is easier to finish off threads than to start them. Unless you can mask a beginning thread with later stitches, or darn it invisibly into the fabric, start with a knot about 5 cm (2 in.) away from where you wish to begin. Later cut off the knot and darn the end in. This will be most easily done with a sharp pointed needle, if possible finer than the blunt one you have been using. Do not try to work the needle through more than every alternate stitch, one at a time, or you may distort the stitch on the surface.

For decorative uses, or dress, do not overlook woollen fabrics. Some contemporary woollen fabrics are very suitable for use in this type of embroidery.

42   Table mats by Muriel Thorn, Melbourne
Simple edges using Danish picot edge

72

Finishing

This is most important. A well-finished article will always attract attention, whilst the very best work badly presented does not do justice to itself. Obviously, the use to which your embroidery will be put will determine how you will finish it. Considerable thought should be given to this before a start is made on the work.

Table linen

Fabrics for table use can vary with the setting in which they will be used, but nothing repays the work that goes into it more than pure linen. Much as we may wish for crease-resistant and minimum-care fabrics, they do not have the durability of pure linen. They are either treated with a resin finish which wears off in time or have a synthetic fibre woven with the linen which lowers the temperature at which the iron may be used and so the finished job does not look as good as pure linen.

It is just one of those decisions that must be made, is the ironing to be a quick and easy job or is the laundered linen to show to its best advantage?

Pressing

This will add so much to the appearance of your work that it is worth taking time and trouble with it. Place your embroidery *face downwards* on a cloth pad. Either damp it in the traditional way by sprinkling it with water and rolling in a towel until it is evenly damp; or cover it with a cloth wrung out in water and press with an iron as hot as the material will stand. Materials containing synthetics need a cooler iron than linen or cotton.

Press from the centre outwards, on the grain, always keeping the edges straight. Good ironing of table linen takes time and care.

43   Table mat by Myrtle Black, Melbourne
Simple geometric design using Danish picot edge, four-sided stitch, pulled satin stitch and ringed back stitch

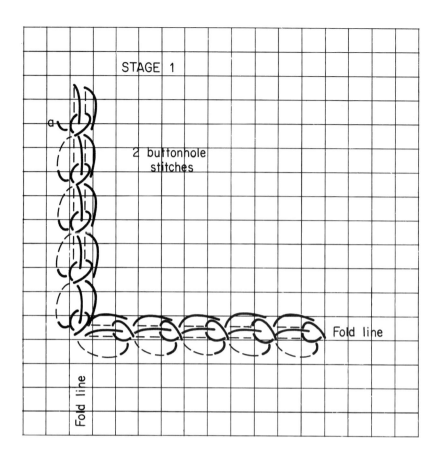

Danish picot edge

This gives a light but very durable finish. It is simply done and very effective although the instructions look lengthy.

Stage 1   1.5 cm ($\frac{1}{2}$ in.) from the edge of the cloth make 2 buttonhole stitches into the same holes over 2, 3 or 4 threads, depending on the coarseness of your material. Pull the stitch tight and the knot well up on top, so that it will show. Do not pull your work so tight that the edge will be puckered. Slide your needle underneath and to the left and bring it out through the material, about level with the bottom of the stitch just made. Repeat as often as necessary.

Stop 1.5 cm ($\frac{1}{2}$ in.) from the corner. Turn your work and continue along the next side in the same manner (see line drawing).

74

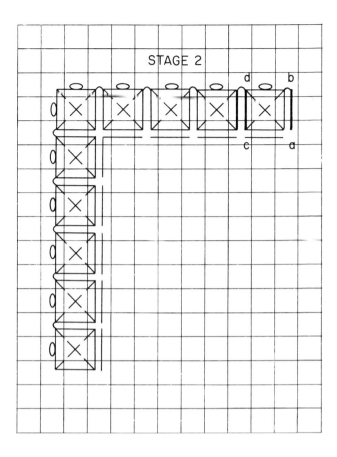

Stage 2 Turn fabric under so that the knots of the previous row form the edge. Follow Stage 2 line drawing. The needle travels from:

a—b, twice these are buttonhole stitches
b—c behind the fabric
c—a
a—c
c—a
a—d behind the fabric
d—c twice these are buttonhole stitches as at
a—b

Repeat as often as necessary.

To turn a corner Stop about 2.5 cm (1 in.) short of the corner. Trim excess linen right back to the stitching which you have just done. Fold second side. Continue stitching to the corner through both layers. Turn corner and proceed until edge is complete *(42)*.

The danish picot edge which looks so fragile *(43)*, in fact, will last as long as the fabric. Once the edge is turned over and stitched there are endless possibilities of adding extra rows as desired. If adding rows of drawn satin stitch to four-sided stitch, do remember that the satin stitch rows should be done before the rows of four-sided stitch. You may need to leave unworked the rows or blocks of four-sided stitch while you do lower rows of satin stitch and then return to finish them.

A very bold border and a very firm one, can be done by using open cross stitch. Start with row 1 and 2 of the danish picot edge and then do a band of open cross stitch as deep as you wish. You will notice that you do the 'up' and 'down' rows before turning your work to do the second stage. *(Stitch no 21.)*

Be careful that the border does not overwhelm the design and stitchery.

75

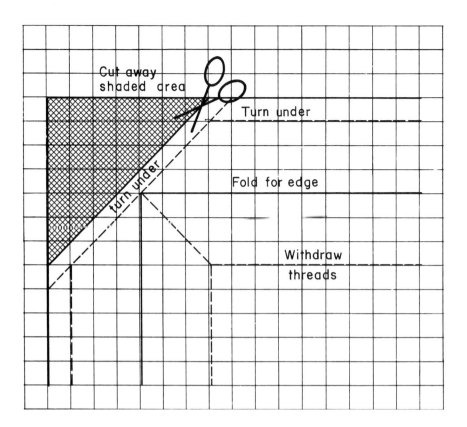

Cut away shaded area

Turn under

Turn under

Fold for edge

Withdraw threads

Mitred corners

The traditional way of hemming linen is where one, or more than one, thread is withdrawn and then the fabric turned under with a narrow folded edge underneath the wider one. The folded edge is sewn onto the edge of the area where the threads have been withdrawn. It is neat and strong. This requires the corners to be mitred. However, the place where the threads have been withdrawn does weaken in time.

Fold the material on the true bias at the point where the corner of your finished article will be. Press this fold firmly but *do not stretch* (see line drawing).

Trim the excess material leaving only about 7 mm ($\frac{1}{4}$ in.) to turn under.

Turn the edge under and slip stitch edges of corner together invisibly. Tack hem securely before stitching.

Panels

Great care must be taken in the working of panels that are to hang free. There must be no tensions in the stitches that will distort the overall shape.

If your embroidery is for exhibition or competition you will want it to look its very best. If it is very textured or has beads incorporated you will not be able to iron it without losing your carefully planned effects. In this case you use rustless pins and carefully stretch it *face upwards* on a board covered with a wet sheet or towel. Cane-ite (straw board) is good for the board because it is soft enough to stick pins into. It should be at least 5 cm (2 in.) larger than your work.

There must be *no* wrinkles in the wet cloth. It will take care and patience to get your embroidery perfectly smooth and true to shape. This is not usually a problem if the work has been worked in a frame. As you control the tension of your stitches and learn and understand the way certain stitches react, the problem of distortion lessens. *Then leave the work to dry.* Do not dry by putting your work near artificial heat. It may take several days but you can see the texture rising on the surface and in this way you get the very, very best from the work and thought you have put into your work. You will realise that the pins must be very close together or you may get a scalloped look to the edge which is fine if that is the look you intended to have, but if it is not, it is calamitous, however not irretrievable. Go back and start the stretching process from the beginning.

When it is dry it may be hung on a rod to hang freely, or it can be stretched taut over a board.

Cushions

In making up cushions with removable covers, the zipper is inserted across the back and not in the edge. This makes the construction much simpler and looks neater.

Cut the material for the back of your cushion 4 cm ($1\frac{1}{2}$ in.) longer than the front but the same width. Cut in half across the width and press 2 cm ($\frac{3}{4}$ in.) hem on each piece across the width.

Insert the zipper between the two hems so that it is completely hidden. For inserting the zipper follow the instructions which come with it. For a perfect result allow an extra 7 mm ($\frac{1}{4}$ in.) in 30.5 cm (12 in.). *Do not stretch fabric onto zipper.*

Inserting the piping

Do this in three steps.

1 Cut a strip of material long enough to go all the way around the cushion plus 7.5 cm (3 in.). The width of your strip depends on the thickness of your piping cord. With the cord folded inside the strip you need 1.5 cm ($\frac{1}{2}$ in.) turning on both edges. Fold in half with the cord inside.

2 Make the piping with a row of stitching in matching thread. Stitch as close as possible to the cord. Do this with a zipper foot (see line drawing).

3 Tack the piping all around the edge of the front of the cushion, on the right side of the embroidered material. The raw edges of the piping and the edges of the cushion should match. Clip the piping to 1.5 mm ($\frac{1}{16}$ in.) from the stitching line at the corners. The cut fabric will open out to allow the piping to sit flat. *There must be no fullness in the piping.*

Where the ends of piping meet pull cord out and cut back enough so that the material overlaps but so that there is no bulk of the cord overlapping. Allow the cord to run back inside casing and bring piping down at an angle (see line drawing).

Stitch a second time on the same line as the stitching of piping cord. Use a matching thread.

Now place the back of the cushion over the front – right sides facing – and tack around the edges. Stitch on previous stitching line.

Cut away a small triangle of material at each corner to eliminate as much bulk as possible at the corners.

Turn the cushion inside out and pull the corners into place. Place the cushion pad inside. (A cushion pad should be slightly larger than the cushion cover, itself.)

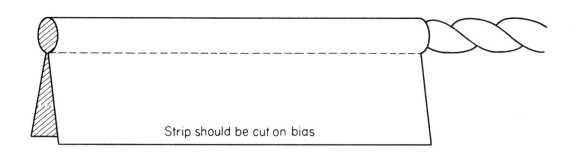

Strip should be cut on bias

Presentation of panels

Free hanging panels

If your work is to hang from a rod you will need either a hem at the top to put a rod through or metal or plastic rings sewn to the edge through which the rod may be inserted.

It may need a lining for neatness. It may be necessary to line your free hanging panel with something slightly darker in tone to give depth and accentuate the lace-like patterns but, then again, if you hang it slightly away from the wall the lacy patterns can throw shadows that add to the interest of your finished work.

Mounted panels

Method 1 Start by stretching your work into shape, if necessary (shown on page 77).

Cut a piece of board the size you wish your finished piece to be. The board should be strong enough to take the stretching load without serious bending.

To begin this method, fix your embroidery by means of pins or drawing pins (thumb tacks), all round the edges of the board.

If you wish your work to have a slightly padded surface, and it does look nicer, place *Dacron* wadding between the embroidery and the board. It may need more than 1 layer of wadding.

If you mark the centres of the sides of your embroidery with coloured thread and draw lines on the back of the mounting board, marking the centres as well, it is much easier to keep your work squared while you are lacing it. If there are straight lines in the weave of your fabric or design you *must* keep them parallel to the edges of the board. *This is very important*.

With strong thread, or fine string, lace from edge to edge across the back starting from the middle and working outwards. Keep your laces

quite close because if far apart, they will pull the fabric into ridges when tightened. You may need to adjust the tension on the strings more than once, until you are satisfied the tension is even.

Finish ends off firmly and do the lacing along the other two sides in the same way. Your lacing should not be so tight that it causes your board to bow.

If you wish to have your work professionally framed this is the stage at which you take it to the framer. This method of presenting embroidery is not much favoured at present and embroidery should not be glazed unless there is some special reason for doing it. So much texture is lost if it is under glass.

A quicker way, but not necessarily a better way, of mounting a panel is to fold it over the board, one side at a time, and hold it in place with adhesive tape. It is very difficult to get any tension onto the material doing it this way.

Method 2 Finished panels look well mounted in front of another, larger, plain coloured board. This second board can be covered with fabric or not as desired. The fabric can be attached to the board in any way which gives a smooth finish.

Here are two ways of attaching the two boards, one to the other.

1 Drill pairs of matching holes in both boards – the holes should be near each corner of the smaller one.

Before starting to lace the embroidery onto the front one, thread strings through the holes in the front board. (The strings should be strong but not bulky and there should be sufficient padding behind the embroidery so that the strings do not show a ridge.) There should be a separate pair of strings for each pair of holes. Leave them hanging behind.

Now complete the instructions for mounting the embroidery on a board. Feed the strings through

the holes in the second board. Tie firmly behind the second board.

2 If you place small blocks of wood, with matching holes, behind your front board, you can feed the strings through these and then through the back board and the front one will stand away from the second.

Method 3 The fabric can be stretched over an artist's stretcher before the work is begun. When the embroidery is finished the work is already mounted and it can be placed in front of another board or hung as it is. Working in this way it is impossible to take the embroidery right to the edge of the fabric, but that may not be a fault (*44*).

44 *White Rythms* 50 × 64 cm (20 × 25 in.)
Wendy Lees, East Molesey, England
Satin stitch, pulled satin stitch, eyelets, and four-sided stitch have been used
Photograph supplied by W Lees

45(a) *Bubbly*   61 × 46 cm (24 × 18 in.)
Edna Wark, Embroiderers' Guild Collection, Melbourne
Photograph by Mary-Ellen Belville

Method 4   The fabric can be stretched over a firm welded wire frame before work is commenced. After the embroidery was completed (*45a and b*) it was left in place and the frame covered with a stretch velvet fabric. The panel was completed with a lining behind the embroidery to give depth and for tidiness. A narrow line of gros grain ribbon was sewn inside the frame.

45(b)   Detail of previous illustration
Covered shapes, beads, sequin rings, variety of threads
were used on a background of white linen scrim.
Polystyrene balls and parts of balls were covered with
very fine linen embroidered in drawn fabric stitches or
detached buttonhole stitch

83

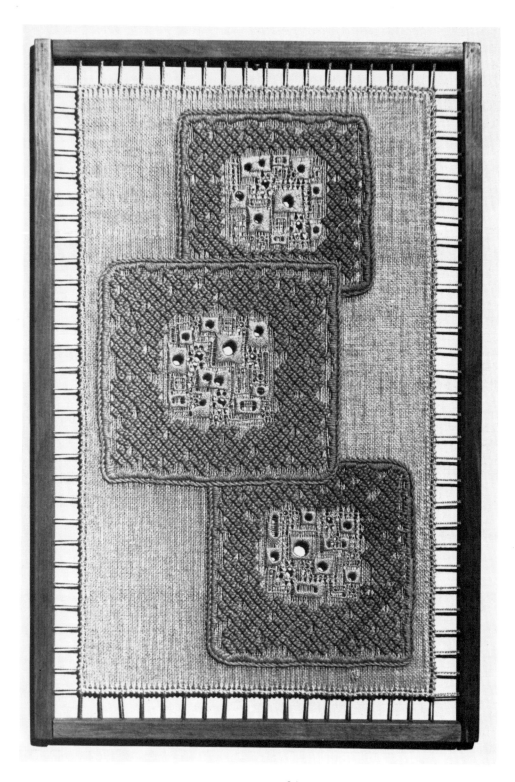

An American method

Embroiderer Nellie Bergh obtains good results 'floating' her drawn fabric panels within a light wooden frame. She finishes her embroidery, completely, using a picot edge then has the frame made a planned size larger with a pre-determined number of small holes drilled in a groove in the sides of the frame. Then she laces the edges of the embroidery through the holes. It is light in weight and very effective (46).

An English method

London Embroiderer Winifred Clayton recently mounted a piece of drawn fabric embroidery and them completely enclosed it in a made-to-measure perspex box. Box and work were only about 2 cm ($\frac{3}{4}$ in.) thick. As the work would be handled a great deal as a demonstration piece this ensures its freshness and cleanliness for all time.

Whichever method you use, hang it so that there is the least distraction to the eye. You want the viewer's eye to be drawn to the embroidery, not the rope which is holding it in place!

46 *Opus 99*
Nellie Bergh, Connecticut, USA
Cream eyelets and Sorbello stitch on cream make this attractive panel with its appearance of 'floating' in its frame
Photograph by Philip Bergh

Conclusion

My acquaintance with drawn fabric embroidery has really grown into a 'love affair'. The deeper I became involved, the more I admired the technical quality of historical pieces.

We cannot hope to rival the gossamer-like qualities of the eighteenth century pieces but we can appreciate the astonishing variety of density and detail which was achieved without varying the working threads. It was all dependent on knowledge of stitch and mastery of tension.

Where do we go from here? Further exploration of base fabrics is always interesting. I feel that hand-knitting as a ground could yield interesting results but so far, the effect that is tantalizing me is still a mirage, not a vision.

If we return to a more disciplined method of working on free-er designs we could find ourselves surprised with the charm and beauty of the result (44). For a description of the development and working of this piece I refer readers to Mrs Lees' own account in the magazine *Embroidery* published for the Embroiderers' Guild, London, Vol. 28 no 1, Spring 1977. For myself, I always feel most at home with a flowing line.

I would like to find a method of sealing finely embroidered table mats between two layers of heat resistant plastic so that they would retain their pristine freshness indefinitely. A plastics firm has told me that it is not satisfactory to embed embroidery in plastic.

This kind of embroidery provides relaxation for the worker because it can be done in the hand quietly and rhythmically and yet is a challenge to one's ingenuity. Surely it must appeal to the same kind of intellect which will find the right word in a crossword puzzle or the fugitive piece in a jigsaw puzzle. There is the same feeling of triumph when the right stitch is found, or developed, for that elusive space.

I am about to start my next piece of drawn fabric embroidery. I hope you are, too, or maybe it is your first excursion into this area? Then good luck with your stitches.

Stitches and how to make them

This is by no means a comprehensive collection of stitches. There are some very basic ones. There are several complicated ones. There are an assortment of stitches based on faggot stitch which suggest how any stitch could be developed. There are some textural stitches to give added interest.

When learning a new stitch be sure to have several different pieces of material and different kinds of threads at hand to see how the stitch reacts to different conditions.

To interpret the line drawings:

Thick lines indicate the stitch or stitches in process of completion.

Thin lines indicate stitches made previously.

Broken lines indicate the thread carried under the material.

Each line of the graph = 1 thread of the material.

In a few cases, a stitch illustration has been greatly enlarged to show it in greater detail and occasionally, a single stitch has been worked over a larger number of threads for the same reason.

Evenness of tension and finally *no* distortion of the overall shape of the fabric, are the hall-marks of expert drawn fabric embroidery.

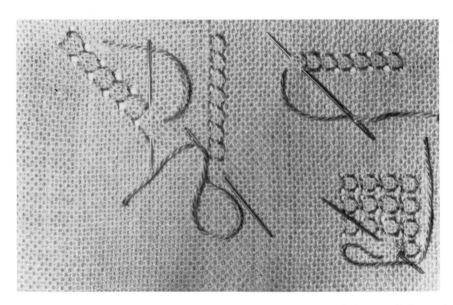

Four-sided stitch (no 1a)

This is a very useful stitch. It can be used as a line stitch, horizontally, vertically or diagonally.

Isolated stitches, in varying sizes, can be used to give a powdered effect. It is useful in borders and blocks. It does not pull the material out of shape. Follow the diagrams, starting at 'a' in all cases.

Ringed four-sided stitch (no 1b)

This stitch has the same advantages as four-sided stitch but gives a lighter appearance. One or two threads can be left between the stitches and rows of stitches.

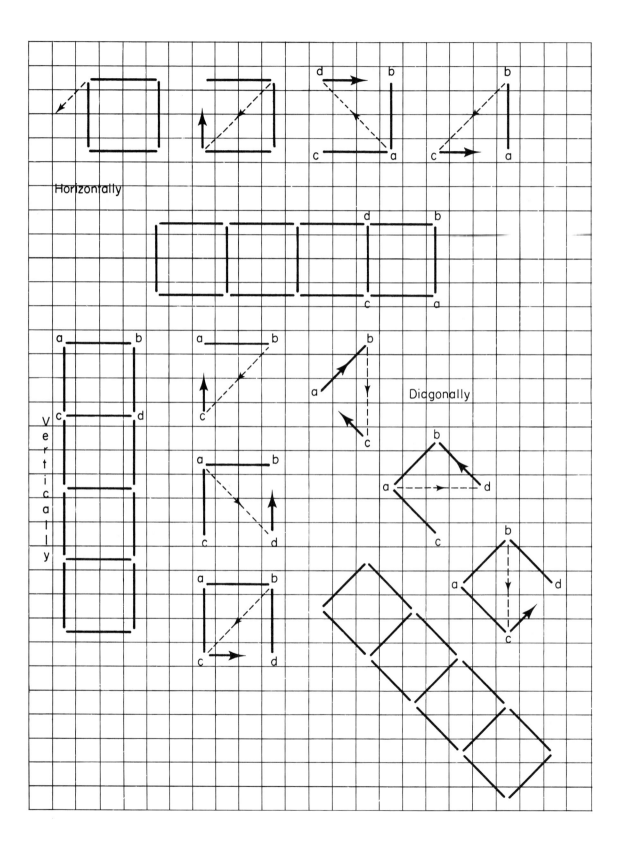

Horizontally

Vertically

Diagonally

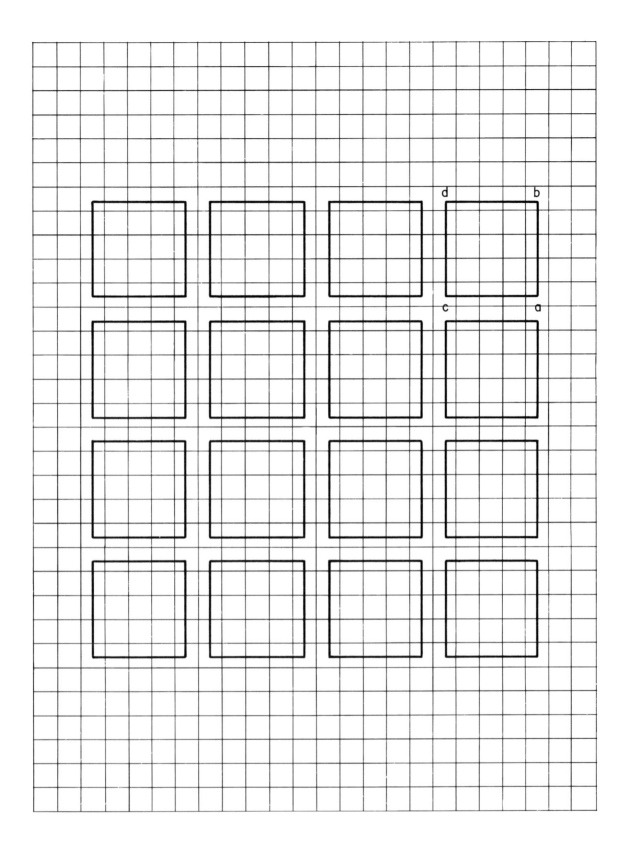

Diagonal cross band (no 2)

This stitch rises diagonally with upright stitches on the surface. The 'cross' is completed on the return journey with horizontal stitches on the surface.

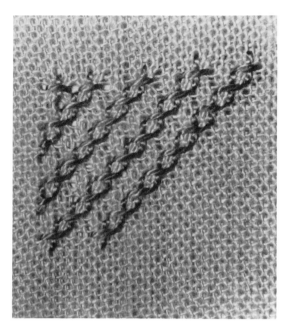

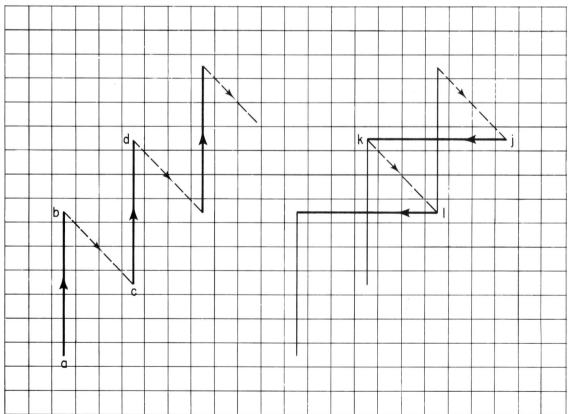

Drawn diagonal ground (no 3)

This stitch is simple and makes an even background. On some fabrics it retains an intriguing tiny square in the centre of the stitch.

Work *right* to *left*. To return reverse the directions.

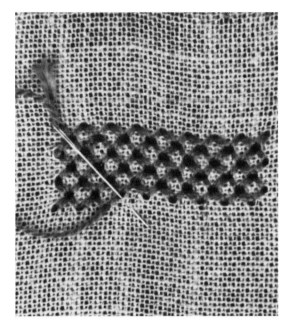

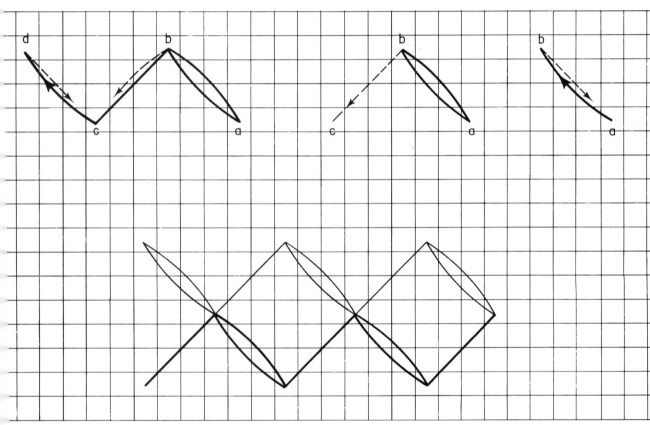

91

Double back stitch (no 4)

This is the reverse side of herringbone stitch. The threads on the back of the material give depth and contrast of tone. The width of the stitch can be varied and makes a whole group of stitches by its changes.

Progress from *right* to *left*, starting at 'a'.

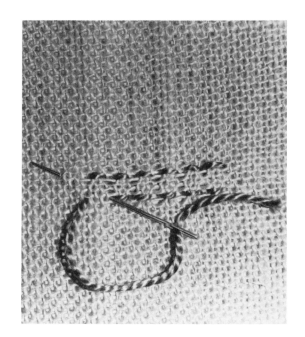

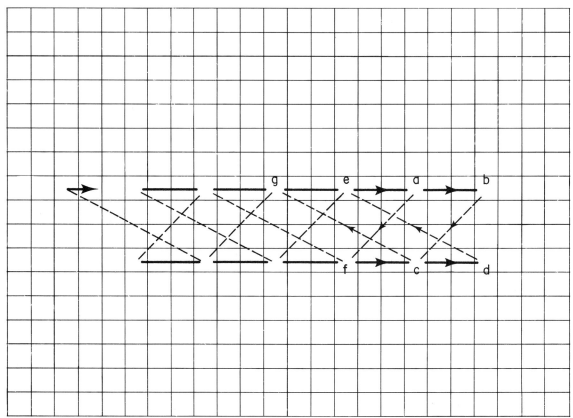

Square stitch (no 5)

When several double back stitches are worked in a horizontal line and then the same number worked in a vertical line within the same area it makes a lozenge shaped area with a precise outline. If the tension is increased these become small cushioned areas and give textural interest.

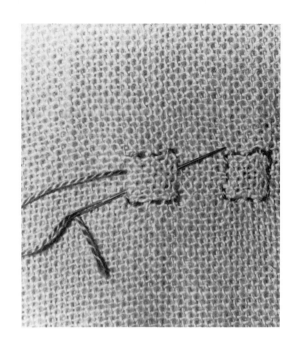

Stage 1 The needle travels from:
a—b
b—c
c—d
d—e
e—a
a—f
f—c
c—g
g—e
e—h
h—f

Stage 2 The needle travels from:
f—i
i—h
h—j
j—d
d—k
k—i
i—l
l—j
j—g
g—k
k—b
b—l

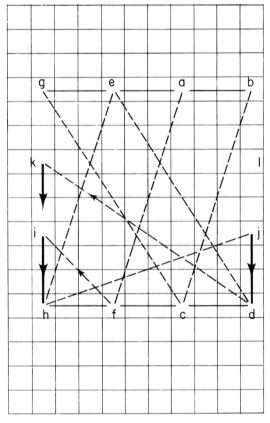

Double stitch (no 6)

This stitch also gives neat rows of stitches on the right side. The stitches are always made in a forward direction and those on the back make a saw-tooth pattern and do not overlap each other. It is much used in Chikan work and Ayrshire work. Work from *right* to *left*.

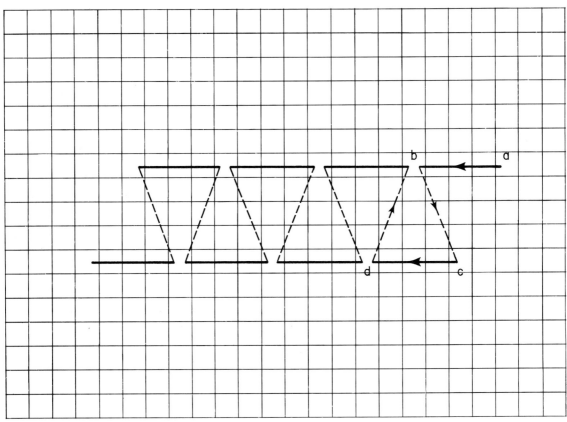

Satin stitch (no 7)

Straight stitches placed close together and covering the grain of the material but which do not overlap each other, are called satin stitch. The stitches may all be the same size or increasing and decreasing on a pre-arranged pattern.

By changing the angle of the stitches great play of light and shade can be obtained. By varying the tension on the stitches variety can also be achieved.

Satin stitch is used to give solidity against lacy areas and shine against matt areas.

Eyelets (no 8)

These are a form of satin stitch worked around a central point. Tension plays a big part here. By increasing the tension on the middle stitch along each side a star effect can be obtained.

Extra rows of pulled satin stitch around the outside of an eyelet add importance to it. Crossed threads can be left in the middle giving another variation. Parts of eyelets can be fitted together to make interesting groupings.

95

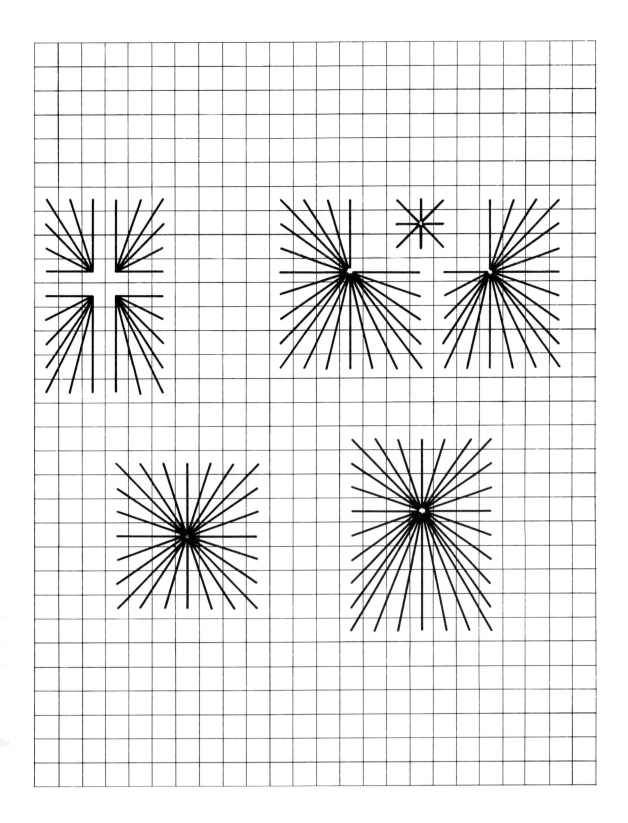

Faggot stitch (no 9)

This stitch makes a good grounding stitch. If used in conjunction with other stitches it makes some interesting variations.

It is worked on the diagonal, descending in steps and then ascending in steps.

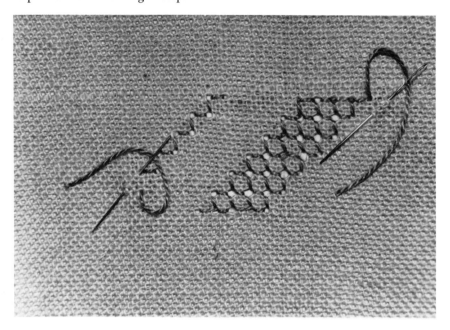

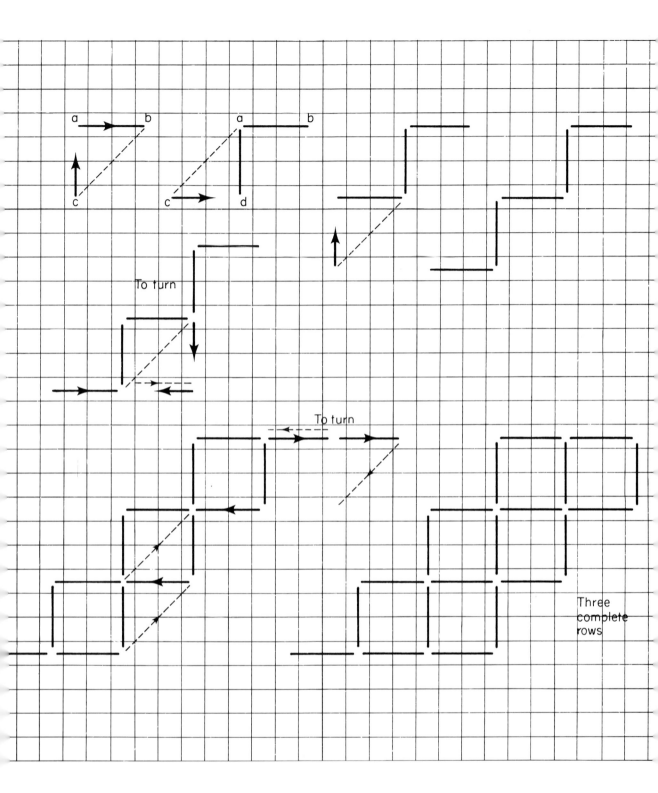

To turn

To turn

Three
complete
rows

99

Reverse faggot stitch (no 10)

As its name implies, this is the stitch which appears on the back of the material when doing faggot stitch.

Work in diagonal lines from *top* to *bottom* and then from *bottom* to *top*.

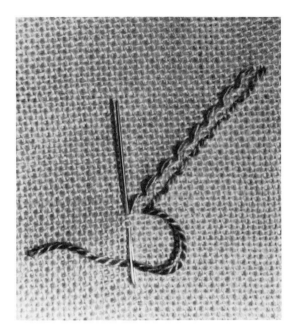

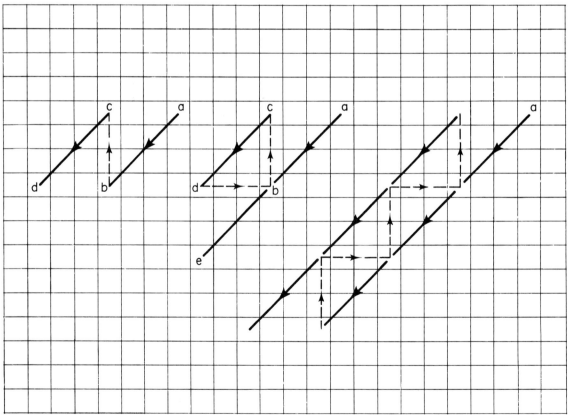

Turkish triangular stitch (no 11)

This stitch is worked on a grounding of faggot stitch.

The second half of the stitch, worked on top of the grounding is reverse faggot stitch.

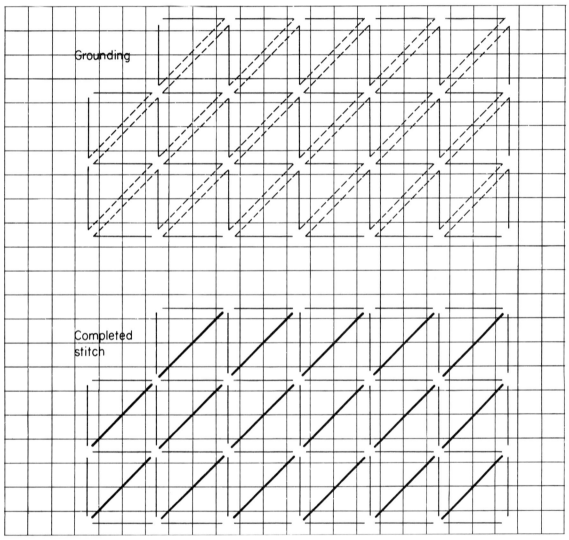

Grounding

Completed
stitch

Diagonal drawn filling (no 12)

This is faggot stitch but leave *one* extra thread between the rows and drop down *one* thread at the beginning of each successive row.

This filling stitch was frequently used in historical pieces for the groundings which look so much like net.

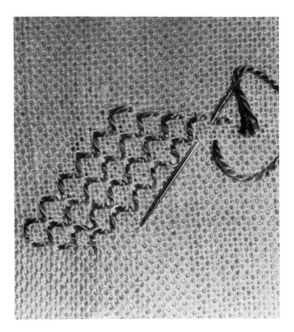

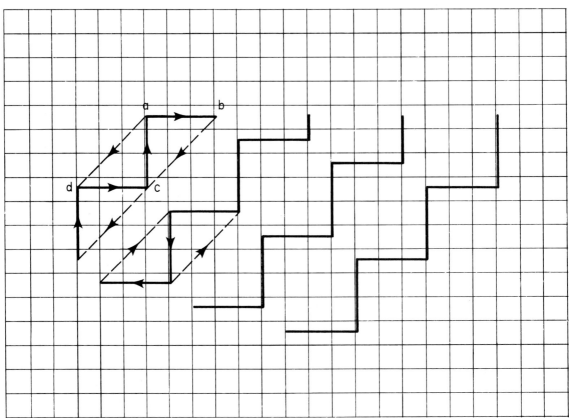

Diagonal chevron stitch (no 13)

Alternating rows of faggot and reverse faggot
stitch are used to make this stitch.

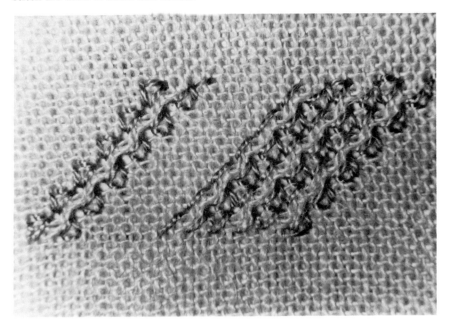

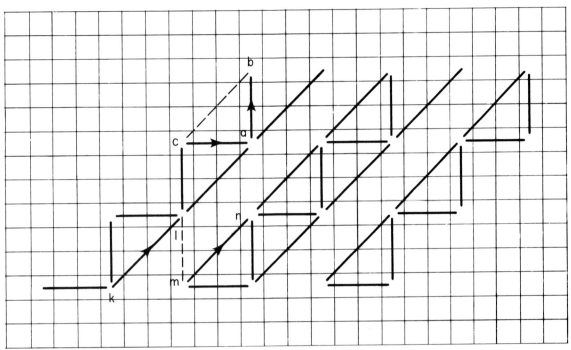

Mushabak stitch (no 14)

This is a Turkish stitch. The method of working is
related to reverse faggot stitch. The counting is
different and it gives a slightly different shape to
the pattern.

Follow the lettering on the line drawing.

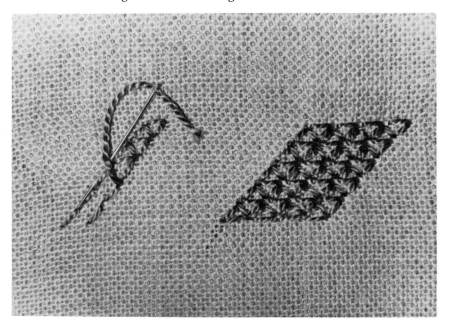

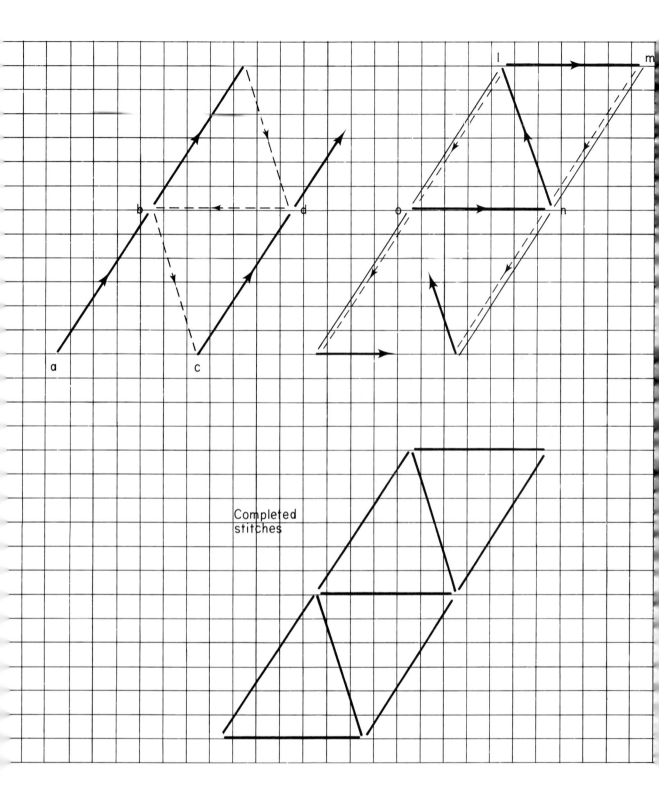

Completed
stitches

Three-sided stitch (no 15)

This stitch is a bit difficult to learn but it makes a
satisfactory grounding stitch used in regular rows.
Used in conjunction with fringe it can be an edge
to table linen.

   Work from *right* to *left*. The needle travels from:

a—b
b—a
a—b
b—c
c—b
b—c
c—b
b—c
c—a
a—c
c—a
a—d
d—a
a—d
d—a
a—d
d—c
c—d
d—c and continue.

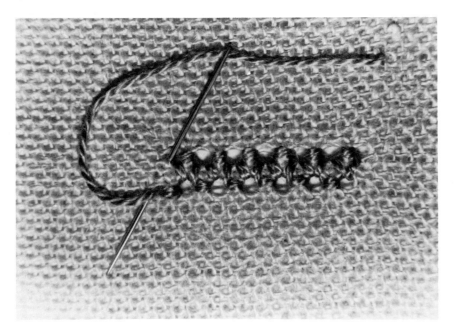

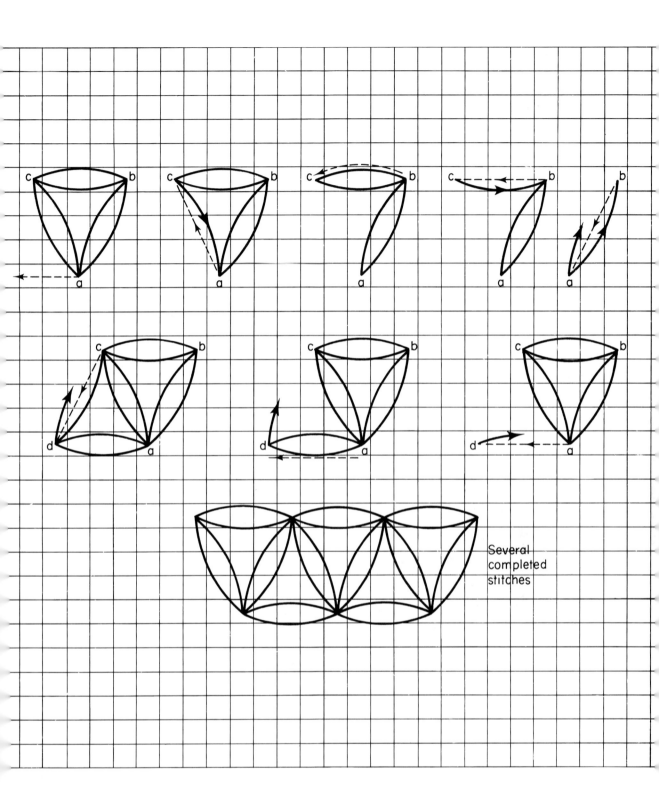

Several
completed
stitches

Eyelet filling (no 16)

This stitch is three-sided stitch worked around a central point.

I think it is easiest to do, if you start each eyelet from the centre. Careful counting is essential. The needle travels from:

a—b
b—a
a—b
b—c
c—b
b—c
c—b
back to a
and repeat

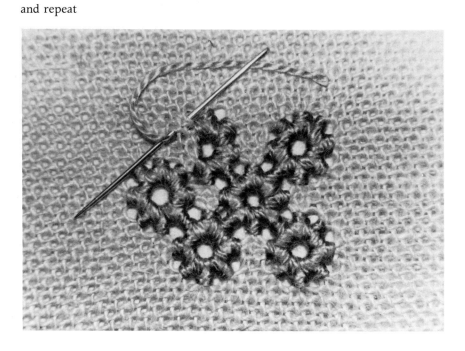

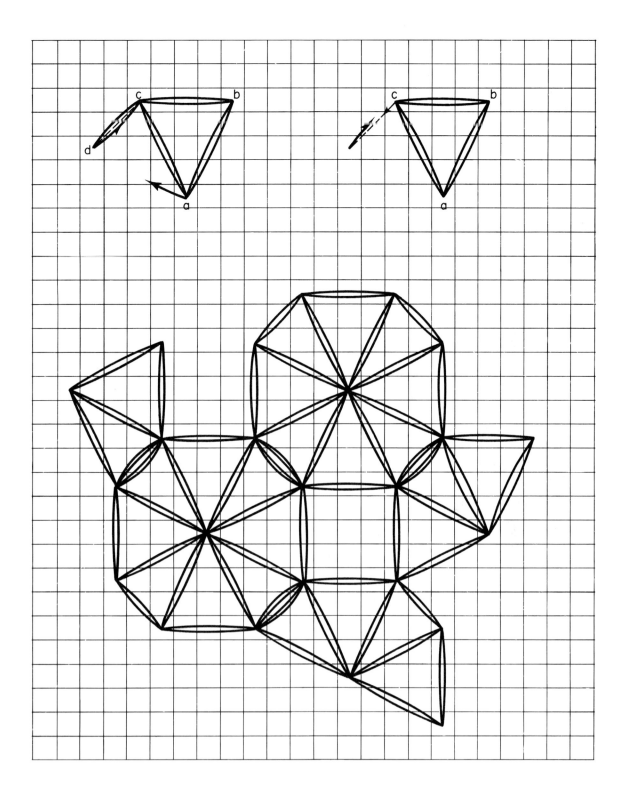

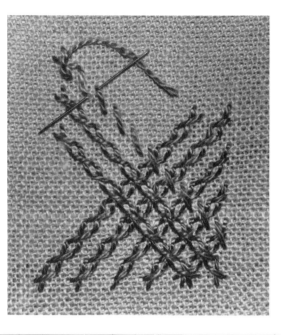

Chequer filling (nos 17a and b)

This is a complicated stitch which requires careful counting.

For *Stage 1* the first row starts in the bottom *left* corner and mounts, in steps, to the right. Complete first row by returning using the same holes, making crosses as you do so.

The second and succeeding rows are worked in similar fashion, starting 8 threads to the *right*.

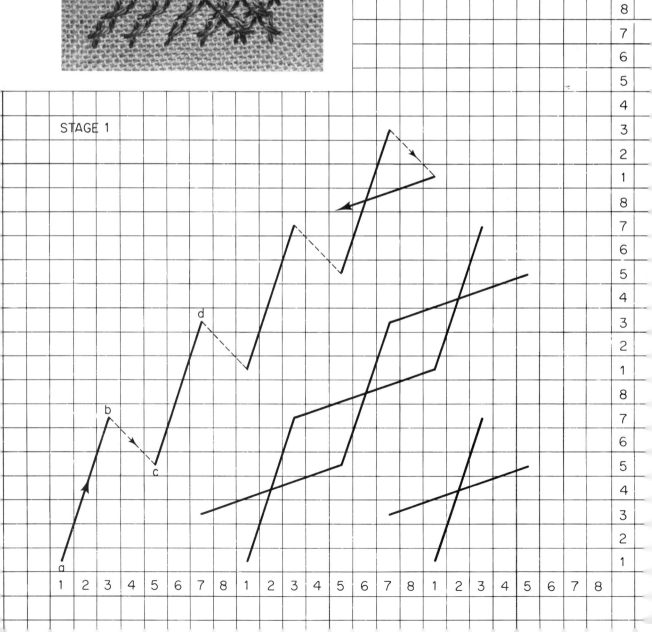

STAGE 1

For *Stage 2*, commence 2 threads to the *right* of the previous stitches in the bottom row and climb upwards to the *left* in the same manner as in *Stage 1*, and back again.

Your threads in each cross all converge on the same centre spot as in *Stage 1* but sloping in the opposite direction.

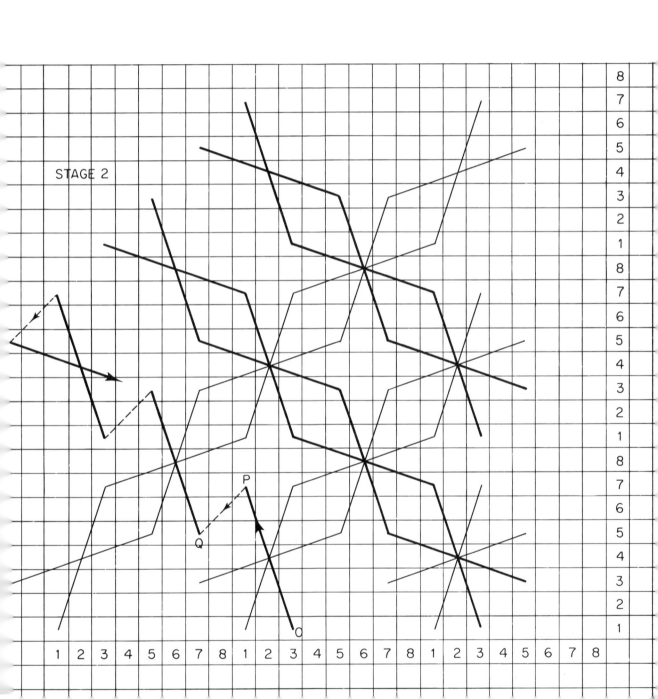

STAGE 2

Mürver stitch (no 18)

This is a Turkish stitch which gives a solid effect on firmly woven fabric but on open weave produces a very open background. In either case it is lovely.

It is worked half going and completed on the return journey. Follow the letters on the line drawing. The only thing to watch for is that the short upright stitches in the first part should hold the crossbar in place and on the return journey the short downward stitch should hold the second crossbar down at the same spot.

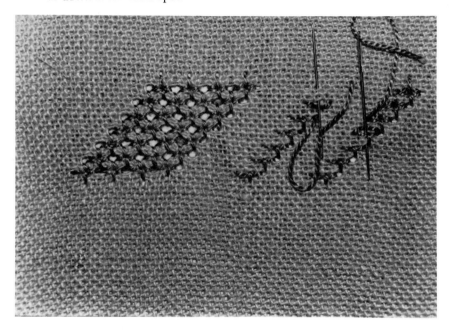

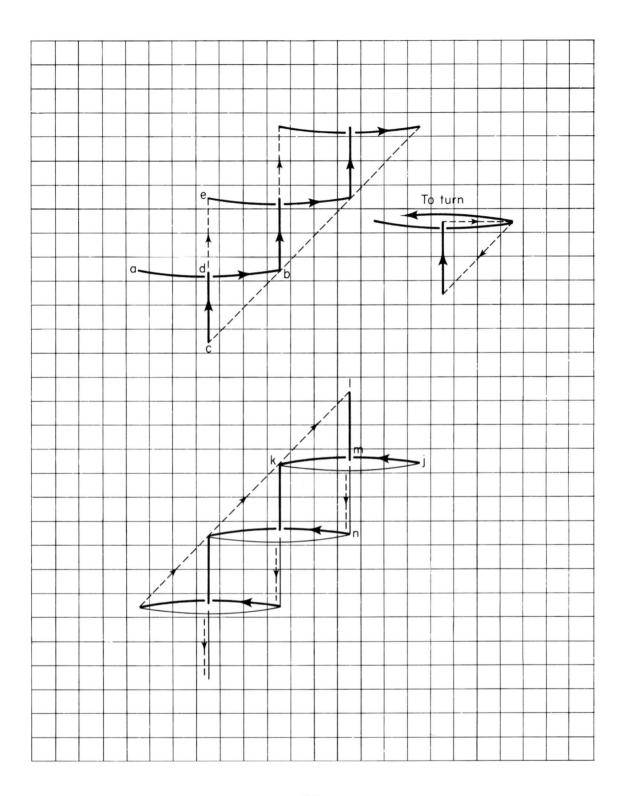

To turn

Squared ground stitch (no 19)

This stitch appears similar to four-sided stitch but has only *one* diagonal thread on the back of each stitch. The stitch is easiest worked on the reverse side of the fabric.

An extra stitch must be added at one end and along the bottom row to complete the grid.

Work from *left* to *right*.

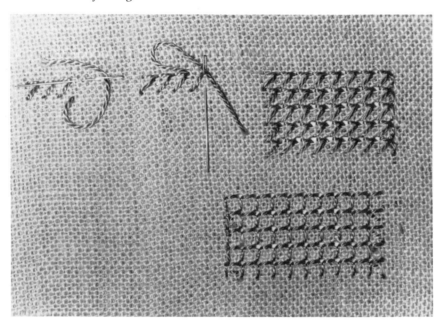

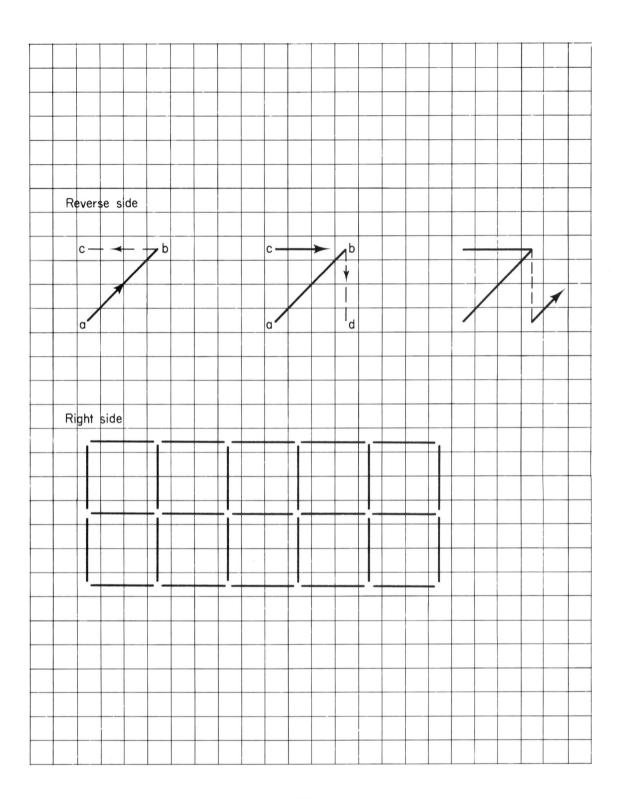

Reverse side

Right side

Greek cross stitch (no 20)

This stitch is made of four buttonhole stitches taken at right-angles to each other.

The threads wrap around each other in the centre and then the tension of the threads pulls the outer ends of the stitch inwards. If the threads do not interlock in the centre an eyelet appears.

If used as a grounding it is easiest done in diagonal rows.

This stitch, worked on loosely woven fabric, pulls the background into a circular design which is more obvious than the crosses. It can be used in conjunction with other stitches.

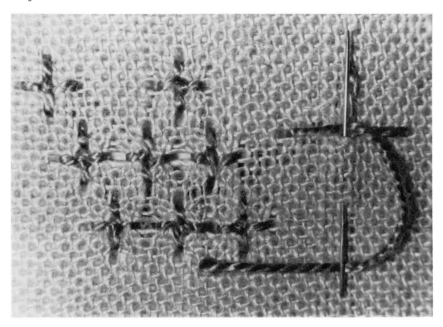

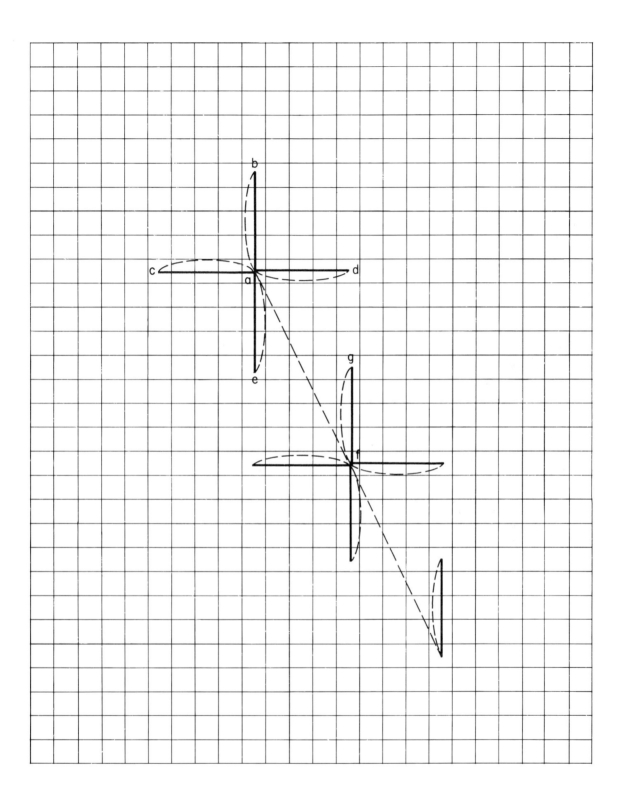

Open cross stitch (no 21)

This stitch is much used in Eastern Mediterranean work. When completed it is difficult to tell the difference between it and two-sided italian cross but the method of working is quite different and, I think, less confusing.

The first stage is worked up from the *bottom* to the *top* and then *down* over the same stitches so that they appear the same front and back.

When all the rows of the first stage have been worked *turn* the work 90° and repeat the first stage so that when you are finished all stitches are crossed on front and back and surrounded by straight stitches.

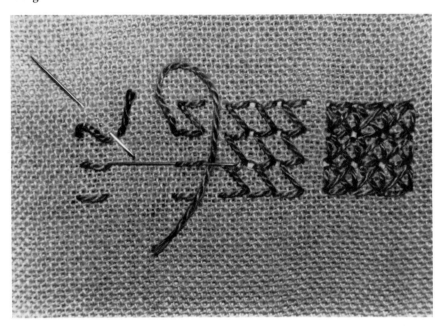

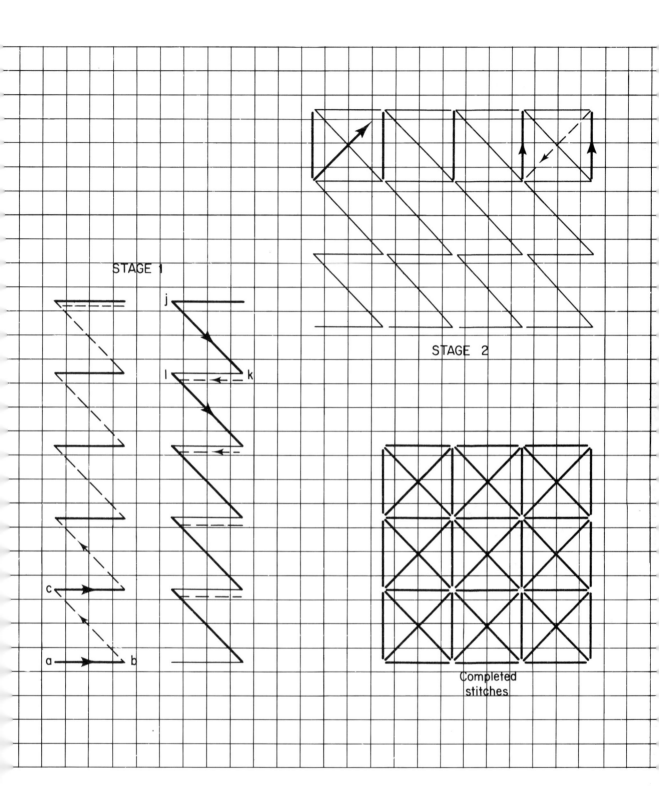

STAGE 1

STAGE 2

Completed
stitches

Raised chain band (no 22)

Make a ladder of stitches. They must be evenly spaced. The thread used for the second stage can be much coarser than the one used for the ladder as the needle and thread slide up and down under the rungs without going through the material except to start and finish.

Having made the ladder, bring the needle out at the top of the ladder 'a'.

Slide the needle *up* under the top rung at 'b'.

Bring the needle back to the centre of the ladder and hold the thread loosely under your left thumb.

Slide the needle *down* under the same rung on the right of centre 'c'. Be sure to bring your needle out over the loop under your thumb. Tighten until the thread sits comfortably, but not too tightly.

This makes the chain stitch. Repeat for each rung of the ladder. Remember, always, to bring your thread back to the centre after each stitch. If the ladder is wide, more than one row may be done side by side or a separate ladder can be built for each row.

The stitch can be quite 'leggy' or really 'chunky' depending on the distance between the rungs of the ladder and the kind of thread used.

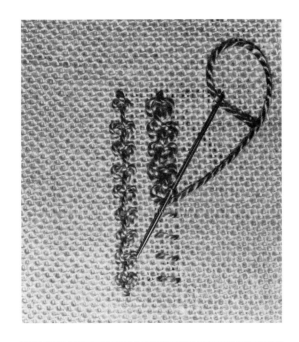

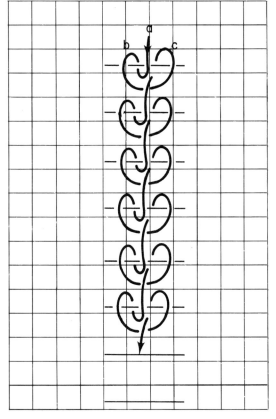

120

Raised stem band (no 23)

Make a ladder similar to the one for raised chain band. Finish off firmly.

Bring the needle out at the *bottom* of the ladder at 'a'.

Climb to the top making a series of stem stitches by slipping the needle *down* under the rungs one at a time. Finish the thread off when you reach the top of the ladder.

Repeat as often as needed to fill the rungs of the ladder with a lovely smooth strip of stitches.

If the strip is to be very prominent, long rows of threads – or even cord – can be placed under the ladder. This raises the rows of stem stitch.

This stitch is much used in Casalguidi work (3).

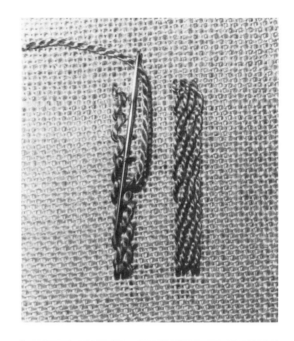

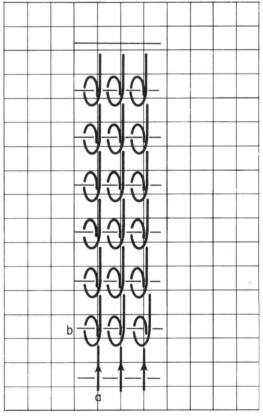

Sorbello stitch (no 24)

A stitch from southern Italy which gives a textured surface. It is not difficult and worked in a coarse twisted thread can be very bold.

It can be used solidly for a background or to make the design stand out conspicuously. Nellie Bergh has worked it diagonally (46), when it is somewhat similar to eastern stitch.

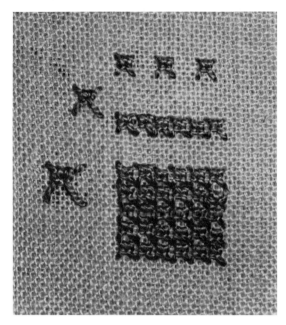

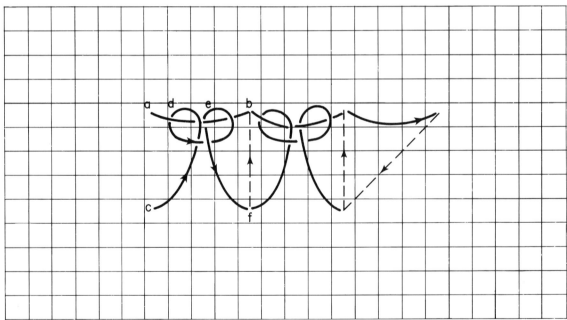

Eastern stitch (no 25)

This is a very old stitch which comes from Egypt. It is slightly different to Sorbello stitch, though quite like a diagonal version of it.

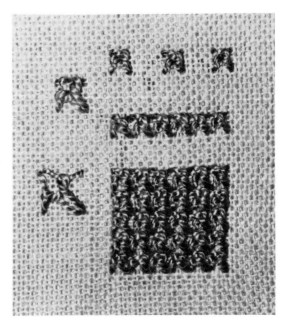

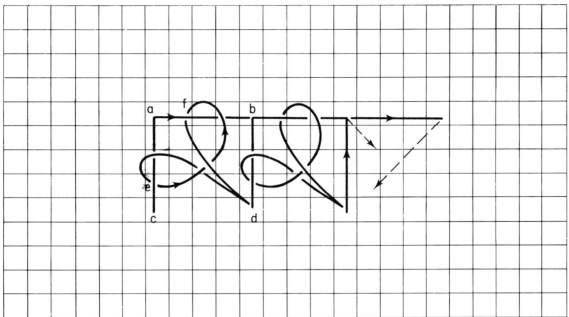

Phanda knot (no 26)

This stitch comes from India where it is an important part of Chikan embroidery.

It is not easy to describe by diagram but the stitch is not difficult to do. The stitches that make the knot all pass through the same hole at the top and at the bottom. Remember that the needle is pulled away from you.

When you wish to make a knot, make a small stitch slanting upwards to the right and bring the needle out directly above it. Pull the needle through.

Bring the needle down under the tiny slanting stitch just made. Do not pull the thread too tight. Make two buttonhole stitches with the needle pointing *away from you*. Take the needle down through the material and this will tie the two stitches down firmly. Bring the needle out at the base of the knot and take a stitch across the bottom of the knot by sliding the needle under the original slanting stitch from *left to right*.

The knots may be close together or isolated. Work from *left* to *right*.

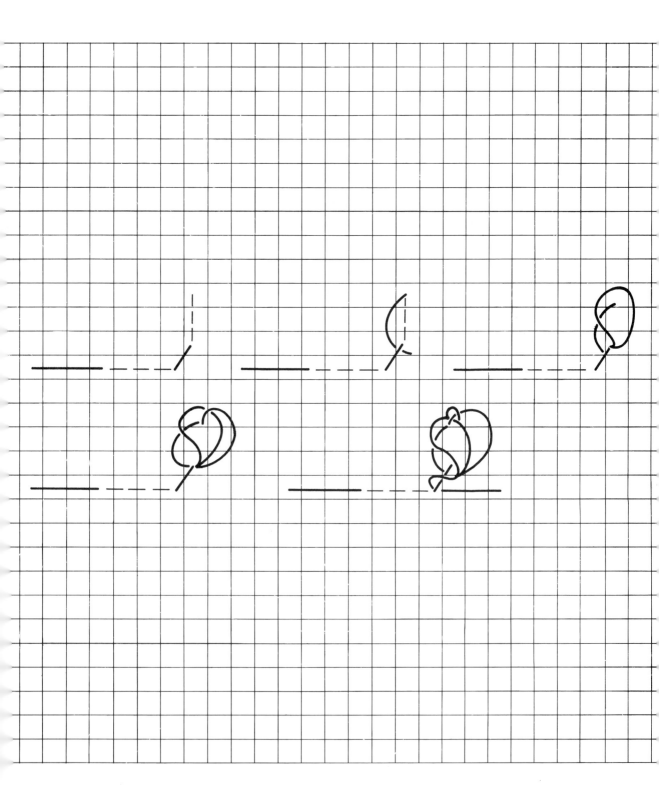

Turkish plate stitch (no 27)

The illustration shows the stitch worked in silver plate where each stitch is finished individually.

When using embroidery cotton or silk work continuously. Pulled very tightly this stitch makes a very open pattern.

Start at 'a' and follow the line drawing. Always work from *right* to *left*.

Size of motif 3.5 cm × 2.5 cm ($1\frac{5}{8}$ in. × 1 in.).

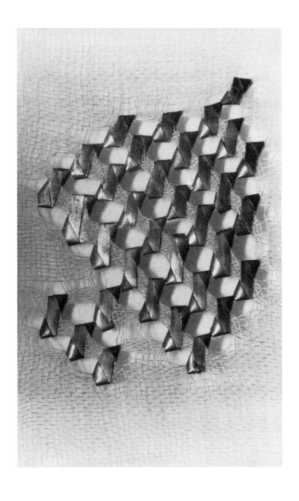

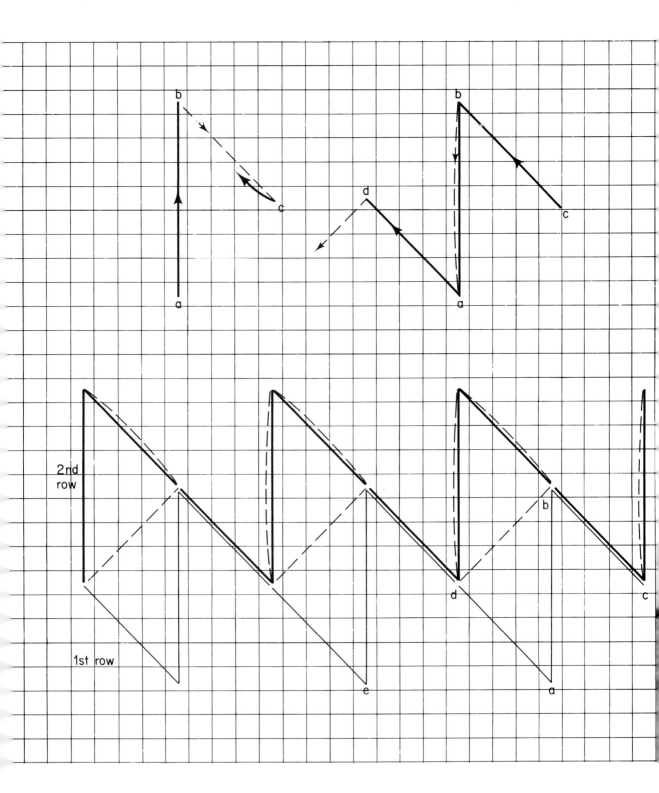

Bibliography

Anchor Manual of Needlework *Batsford, London, 1968*
Linen Embroidery ETTA CAMPBELL *Batsford, London, 1957*
Samplers and Stitches MRS A CHRISTIE *Batsford, London, 1920, 1985*
Encyclopèdie des Ouvrages des Dames T DE DILLEMONT *Dolfus, Mieg and Co, Dornach, Alsace*
Pulled Thread I ESTHER FANGEL *Handarbejdets Fremmes Forlag, Copenhagen, 1958*
Pulled Thread II FANGEL, WINCKLER AND MADSEN *Handarbejdets Fremmes Forlag, Copenhagen, 1958*
Indian Embroideries MRS K M HARRIS *The Embroideress, No 50, 1934*
Indian Embroideries J IRWIN AND J HALL *Calico Museum, Ahmedabad, 1973*
Drawn Fabric Embroidery AGNES LEACH *Halton and Co, London, 1959*
A Complete Guide to Drawn Fabric KATE LOFTHOUSE *Pitman, London, 1951*
Handcrafts and Industrial Arts of India RUSTAM J MEHTA *1960*
Masterpieces of Indian Textiles RUSTAM J MEHTA *D B Taraporevala and Sons, Bombay, 1970*
Pulled Thread MOYRA MCNEILL *Bell & Hyman, London, 1986*
Descriptive Catalogue of the Lace and Embroideries in the South Kensington Museum
    MRS F B PALLISER *1881*
The Art of Embroidery M SCHUETTE AND MÜLLER-CHRISTENSEN (TRANSLATED BY DONALD
    KING) *Thames and Hudson, London, 1964*
Turkish Embroidery GÜLSEREN RAMAZANIGLU *Van Nostrand Reinhold, New York, 1976*
Embroidery Stitches BARBARA SNOOK *Dryad Press, London, 1985*
Mediterranean and Near Eastern Embroideries A J B WACE *Halton and Co, London, 1935*
The Constance Howard Book of Stitches *Batsford, London, 1979, 1985*

Museums and collections

(It is advisable to check dates and times of opening locally)

Benaki Museum, 1 Odos Koumbari, Athens, Greece
Embroiderers' Guild, Apartment 41, Hampton Court Palace, East Molesey, Surrey, KT8 9AU
Embroiderers' Guild of Australia, 170 Wattletree Road, Malvern, Melbourne, Australia 3144
    (Appointment needed to see collection)
Industrie-und-Gewerbe-Museum, 2 Vadian Strasse, St Gall, Switzerland
Kunstindustrimuseet, 68 Bredegade, Copenhagen, Denmark (Opens 1 pm)
National Gallery of Victoria, 180 St Kilda Road, Melbourne, Australia (Closed Mondays)
Platt Hall, Platt Fields, Platt Lane, Manchester, England
Topkapi Palace Museum, Istanbul, Turkey
Victoria and Albert Museum, South Kensington, London (Closed Fridays)

Suppliers

Great Britain

Embroidery threads and accessories
Mary Allen
Turnditch, Derbyshire

E J Arnold and Son Limited
(School Suppliers)
Butterley Street
Leeds LS10 1AX

Art Needlework Industries Limited
7 St Michael's Mansions
Ship Street
Oxford OX1 3DG

The Campden Needlecraft Centre
High Street
Chipping Campden
Gloucestershire

Craftsman's Mark Limited
Broadlands, Shortheath
Farnham, Surrey

Creative Crafts
11 The Square
Winchester SO23 9ES

Dryad (Reeves) Limited
Northgates
Leicester LE1 4QR

B Francis
4 Glenworth Street
London NW1

Fresew
97 The Paddocks,
Stevenage
Herts SG2 9UQ

Louis Grossé Limited
36 Manchester Street
London W1 5PE

Handweavers Studio
29 Haroldstone Road
Walthamstow, London E17 7AN

The Handworkers' Market
The Shire Hall
Shire Hall Plain
Holt
Norfolk NR25 6BG

Harrods Limited
London W1

Levencrafts
23 Chaloner Street
Guisborough, Cleveland TS14 6QD

Mace and Nairn
89 Crane Street
Salisbury, Wiltshire SP1 2PY

MacCulloch and Wallis Limited
25–26 Dering Street
London W1R 0BH

Christine Riley
53 Barclay Street
Stonehaven, Kincardineshire AB3 2AR

Royal School of Needlework
25 Princes Gate
Kensington SW7 1QE

J Henry Smith Limited
Park Road, Calverton
Woodborough, nr Nottingham

Mrs Joan L Trickett
110 Marsden Road
Burnley, Lancashire

USA and Canada

Embroidery threads and accessories
Appleton Brothers of London
West Main Road
Little Compton
Rhode Island 02837

American Crewel & Canvas Studio
164 Canal Street
PO Box 453
Canastota, NY 13032

Bucky King Embroideries Unlimited
Box 124c, King Bros
3 Ranch, Buffalo Star Rkc
Sheriden, Wyoming 82801

Casa de las Tejedoras
1618 East Edinger
Santa Ana, California 92705

Craft Kaleidoscope
6412 Ferguson Street
Indianapolis 46220

Dharma Trading Company
1952 University Avenue
Berkeley, California 94704

Folklorico Yarn Co
522 Ramona Street
Palo Alto 94301, California

The Golden Eye
Box 205
Chestnut Hill, Massachusetts 02167

Head and Tails
River Forest
Illinois 60305

Lily Mills
Shelby, North Carolina 28150

One Stitch at a Time
Box 114
102A Main Street
Picton
Ontario KOK 2TO, Canada

Threadbenders
2260 Como Avenue
St Paul, Minnesota 55108

The Thread Connection
1020 East Carson Street
Pittsburgh
Pennsylvania 150203

The Thread Shed
307 Freeport Road
Pittsburgh, Pennsylvania 15215

Yarn Bazaar
Yarncrafts Limited, 3146 M Street
North West Washington DC

Yarn Depot
545 Sutter Street
San Francisco 94118, California

Australia

Australian Capital Territory
Games N'Stitches
21 Bailey Corner
Canberra City, 2601
ACT

Phillip Craft Supplies
53 Colbee Court
Phillip, 2902
ACT

The Silver Thimble
12 Samson Place
Kambah, 2902
ACT

New South Wales
Broadway Needlecraft
St Andrew's Arcade
Town Hall
Sydney, 2000
NSW

The Crewel Gobelin
680 Pacific Highway
Killara, 2071
NSW

The Embroiderer
52 Erskine Street
Sydney, 2000
NSW

Mosman Needlecraft
153 Middle Head Road
Mosman, 2088
NSW

Needlecraft International
19 Railway Parade
Eastwood, 2122
NSW

Simply Stitches
162 Victoria Avenue
Chatswood, 2067
NSW

Stadia Handcrafts
85 Elizabeth Street
Paddington, 2021
NSW
Tues. to Sat. 10 am to 5 pm

Queensland
Hardie's Handcrafts
144 Adelaide Street
Brisbane, 4000
Queensland

Heirloom Crafts
2034 Logan Road
Upper Mt Gravatt, 4122
Queensland

Kit, Krafts & Gifts
Shop 4
Hartley Building
80 Jephson Street
Toowong, 4066
Queensland

Far North Queensland
Nimble Fingers
65 Main Street
Atherton, 4883
Queensland

Richardson's Fabrics
194b Mulgrave Road
Westcourt
Cairns, 4870
Queensland

South Australia
Arty and Crafty
2 West Parkway
Colonel Light Gardens
Adelaide, 5041
South Australia
Phone for an appointment,
277 3763

Blackwood Crafts
243 Main Road
Blackwood, 5051
South Australia

Cottage Crafts
462 Fullarton Road
Myrtle Bank, 5064
South Australia

Needleworld
109 King William Road
Hyde Park, 5061
South Australia

Stitchery Doo
Shop 5
Goodwood and Cross Road
Cumberland Park, 5051
South Australia

Tasmania
From Lois with Love
111 Elizabeth Street
North Hobart, 7000
Tasmania

Joan Horwood Interiors
105 York Street
Launceston, 7250
Tasmania

The Lantern Gallery
1a Beach Road
Kingston Beach, 7151
Tasmania

Little Stitches
Shop 5
Bay Arcade
Sandy Bay, 7005
Tasmania

Mowbray Fabrics and Crafts
276 Invermay Road
Mowbray, 7248
Tasmania

The Needlewoman
Channel Court
Kingston, 7150
Tasmania

The Needlewoman
63 Melville Street
Hobart, 7000
Tasmania

The Patch Works
91 Patrick Street
Hobart, 7000
Tasmania
10 am–4 pm Wed., Thurs., Fri.

Petit Point
57 George Street
Launceston, 7250
Tasmania

Snippets
319 Elizabeth Street
Hobart, 7000
Tasmania

Clifton Joseph
391–393 Little Lonsdale Street
Melbourne, 3000
Victoria

Country Women's Association
3 Lansell Road
Toorak, 3142
Victoria

The Embroidery Den
350a Bay Street
North Brighton, 3186
Victoria

Gabriel Needlework
Suite 1
1st floor
Block Arcade
Collins Street
Melbourne, 3000
Victoria

Handcraft House
200 Glenferrie Road
Malvern, 3144
Victoria

Twinecraft
89–93 Whitehorse Road
Deepdene, 3103
Victoria

Wondoflex
1353 Malvern Road
Malvern, 3144
Victoria

New Zealand

The Craft Shop
33 Picton Street
Howick
Auckland

The Embroiderer
142a Hinemoa Street
Birkenhead
Auckland

Greensleeves
Campbells Building
Cnr Vulcan Lane & High Street
Auckland

Jonora Needlecraft
61 Upper Queen Street
Auckland

Victoria
Bargello Needlework Supplies
819 Glenferrie Road
Hawthorn, 3122
Victoria

Index

Numerals in *italics* refer to illustrations